HEY SUESS!
I AM Oh, OH goD!

HEY SUESS!
I AM Oh, OH goD!

BY: a girl named SUESS

iUniverse, Inc.
New York Lincoln Shanghai

HEY SUESS! I AM Oh, OH goD!

Copyright © 2005 by a girl named SUESS

All rights reserved. No part of this book may be used or reproduced by any means, graphic, electronic, or mechanical, including photocopying, recording, taping or by any information storage retrieval system without the written permission of the publisher except in the case of brief quotations embodied in critical articles and reviews.

iUniverse books may be ordered through booksellers or by contacting:

iUniverse
2021 Pine Lake Road, Suite 100
Lincoln, NE 68512
www.iuniverse.com
1-800-Authors (1-800-288-4677)

ISBN-13: 978-0-595-37775-6 (pbk)
ISBN-13: 978-0-595-82151-8 (ebk)
ISBN-10: 0-595-37775-0 (pbk)
ISBN-10: 0-595-82151-0 (ebk)

Printed in the United States of America

DediCATiON

I am Oh, OH goD. (That's I am 40, Oh God for those of us who are reflective, associative, and refractive. And that's "O O God" for those who read between the lines.) Either way, here it is. STart at the back with the foreword and follow the rainbow. Read eaCH Chapter from the opening, and I will meet you in the middle when you STart over aGAIN AT the beginning. See you when you get there. I hope you are in that number.
tHIS ONE goes out to the ONE I love; tHIS ONE goes out to the one I've left behind.
I want to dediCATe this book to all the BlUe CHILDren in the world. For without BlUe, all the coloUrs of the rainbow wouldn't be tHERE. Without BlUe there would be no green and no purple and no coloUrs in between. All tHERE would be would be red and yellow, black and white. And we All know that SOME thing'S r not black & white. I also want to dedicate tHIS book to my family, each and everY ONE of them in my GENEtic tree. I DO not want to leave one person out. tHAT's O-U-TOO when you read it both ways and STart over again. That's A-GAIN. I want erevyONE in the wolrd to know they CAN make a dffireecne and EACH dffireecne makes US all ONE. ONE 4 ALL, ALL 4 1 + that's ALL.
MAy GOD Bless Y-ou and Shine HIS face Upon YOU ALL; YES even YOU and ESPecially Y-OU.

AG irl nAMed JESS.

Contents

Chapter 4: "G" Is For Green
            Designer Genes 1

Chapter 5: "I" Is For INDIGO
            Late Bloomers, Eventual Genius': Make Sense 9

            "V" Is For VIOLET
            Colorful Collection Of Pictures & Poems 17

            A FINAL NOTE about the author:
            "B" Is For Blue 39

Chapter 3: "Y" Is For YELLOW
            "Y" Everyone Should Be "Seen & Heard";
            Everyone Has A Choice: Now U C "Y" 82

Chapter 2: "O" Is For ORANGE
            My Visit To The Doctor 90

Chapter 1: "R" Is For RED
            Decoding The Language 97

Foreword 101

Chapter 4: "G" Is For Green

Designer Genes

Lured by the anticipation of "making a perfect baby," "improving an offspring looks," or "increasing a child's intelligence," genetic engineering is becoming an increasingly popular idea to a lot of people. The idea is to genetically manipulate or enhance the chromosomes by deleting, adding, or modifying genes thereby producing proteins in such a way as to alter their DNA sequence. Scientists have already accomplished these feats with pine trees, tomatoes, wheat, and salmon. Ethical guidelines prohibit such direct engineering of genes at present; however, there are reports of a New Jersey clinic performing invitrofertilization on fifteen women with their own egg, mate's sperm, and a small amount of a third party's egg. This was done in the spring of 2001 and at least two of the reported pregnancies carried genetic material from all three donors. Transgenic animals and crops are already in existence. Embryonic stem cells growing in a tissue culture with the preferred DNA as well injecting a chosen gene into the pronucleus of a fertilized mouse egg are already commonly employed. Corn and soybean fields have been planted with transgenic seed since the middle of the 1990's.
Somatic gene therapy and germline genetic engineering are two current methods that we have in order to change human genes. There have been reports of cloning, but to date there is controversy on whether or not a human has been cloned; such a baby would probably become government property if proven. In somatic gene therapy, the genes of somatic cells can be manipulated in order to modify the disease of an individual. A genetically inherited disease can be prevented in offspring as well when germ cells are modified; the entire descendent line is then changed forever since modification of genetic DNA leads to changes both in the structure, the composition, and the amounts of proteins it

eventually produces. Lung, liver, endothelial, white blood and cancer cells are some of the cells targeted in fighting disease. With germline engineering, the idea is to eliminate "stupid," "ugly," or "undesired" people; the experiments are already being conducted extensively with animals in the research field. My personal dilemma with that particular line of "logic" is the researchers who are "creating" people such as themselves; who is at liberty to say that someone is "stupid," "smart," "beautiful," or "ugly"? After all, isn't "beauty in the eye of the beholder"? Isn't "stupid is as stupid does"? Or is that only what a stupid man says?

Another problem with "designer babies" is that once you change the gene sequence in order to attain the "desired genes," you alter other genes as well in the sequence; in a more direct approach, it is highly plausible that you can end up with "a musician who has a fatal childhood leukemia." All the manipulation in the world will not guarantee the "perfect child." In order to get all the genes perfect would fall in line with a quest to become "God." We were created in His image, but we can never achieve such perfectness. To achieve certain wanted genes, other genes **must** be comprised; also, the likelihood of creating new disease exists. Then, we must realize that even then DNA is not written in stone.

DNA can be changed as a result of one's diet, climate, environment, viruses, radiation, and medications as well as unknown causes; the choices we ultimately make affect our very own DNA. Never will there be a 100% guarantee of a "perfect human." To believe such dreams in reality is insanity. We must have a combination of all DNA in order to survive; the good must be taken with the bad. If we continue the trend in such beliefs, we will become extinct as a human race by essentially eliminating so-called "bad genes." Those genes that we are disposing of may be the very genes that create the next "Einstein." To eliminate such genes, for instance, that cause autism or Trisomy 21 may be eliminating essential genes that create specific neural pathways that produce very gifted children. When the DNA proteins are changed, the neural pathways or the wiring of the brain is forever altered as well.

In my opinion, those who have been labeled by others with such "disorders" and "disabilities" are not only "genius" in the fact that they possess an alternative wiring diagram in their brain, but also they subtly and perhaps without a conscious effort prove the rest of us to be unintelligent. We must as a human race start realizing that we all have remarkable abilities no matter what chromosomes we possess, what diseases we have, what genes we hold, or what we look like as an individual. The relevancy here is that "all people are created equal" and "all people were created in the image of God." No one race is superior and no one gene is superior; our eventual fate lies within the choices that are made for us and by us. Everyone counts, even the blue ones.

Ecclesiastes 3:1-8 reads, *"To everything there is a season, and a time to every purpose under heaven: A time to be born, and a time to die; a time to plant, and a time to pluck up that which is planted; A time to kill, and a time to heal; a time to break down, and a time to build up; A time to weep, and a time to laugh; a time to mourn and a time to dance; A time to cast away stones, and a time to gather stones together; a time to embrace, and a time to refrain from embracing; A time to get, and a time to lose; a time to keep, and a time to cast away; A time to rend, and a time to sew; a time to keep silence, and a time to speak; A time to love, and a time to hate; A time of war, and a time of peace.* This quotation from the Bible makes it very clear that we must have a balance in all things; existence won't be possible with the elimination of one or the other. We all must coexist together; after all, the Bible does read, *"Wherever two or more are gathered in My name, I am present."* God cannot possibly exist without the two of us coexisting: the good and the bad; the beauty and the beast; and the talents of all kinds. It takes two to make a thing go right. 2=1

There is nothing like one of us waiting until the last minute. How does one of us determine that the other has waited until the last minute? It appears to me that when you arrive at the last minute and all efforts have virtually been exhausted already before you arrived that <u>you in fact</u> are the one who has procrastinated and in a lame effort to "save face" you place blame on the poor soul who has carried the burden thus far. I believe that instead of "saving face" you have embarrassed yourself beyond belief and you have shown the greatest sign of weakness. People who biologically portray family members in my family have indeed behaved in such manners. I used to make excuses for them, but I finally decided to let them have the responsibility they deserve for their own actions. When I do this, I have found that I am no longer a scapegoat and I get the credit that I deserve, as do those family members that I am referencing. The idle threats of "if you don't do as I say, I will just do this or that," no longer have any power over me. My abusive, controlling husband used to treat me that way and I finally realized that the old wise saying, "People tend to seek out and marry people who are just like their parents," is in fact true. We tend to attract people who are similar to our own DNA. The trick here is to find and associate with people who are like you in many ways yet differ from the rest of your gene line.

In my genes, it is obvious that I donate some of the extra genes that are discarded and not normally donated in the making of a baby. All three of my girls are clones. I see a natural cloning process has occurred with my girls. We look alike, act alike, eat alike, and even talk alike. One day while I was driving down the road, we all spoke at the same time and out of our mouths came the same words and the same sentences. We think alike so much that we can read each other's minds in the same manner that identical multiples do. Some people say that those are just dominant genes, but they are right and wrong. Right because our genes are very dominant, but wrong because of some research and trials that I have done. Most twins or multiples that are considered identical will often say they think that they do not look alike to each other even though they are almost impossible for others to discriminate. Likewise, a true clone will think and look like the other and in fact may be confused because they see themselves. My girls look at pictures of each other and cannot determine that is their sister. My 7 year old argues steadfastly that photographs of my 18 year old are she and insists she does not remember the other items in the picture. She swears they are photos taken of her when she was little when in fact they are not. All four of us girls think and believe the same way; what makes us different in our DNA since our birth is the choices we have made in our lives in regards to diet, exercise, environment, and the like. I am convinced that if all factors while gestating and after birth were identical and the circumstances could be the same, then we would be true walking multiples born years apart.

Twins are an example of "natural cloning" and people continuously ask if my two youngest girls are twins. Some recent experiments with my own family members proved that they cannot determine the difference either and they have even sworn to the identity of the wrong child. As for my husband and myself, we have both even called each of our children the others name numerous times. My husband admits that Karla Michelle (who is not his biological child) looks like our two girls. Karla Michelle's biological father admits the same and appears a bit shocked. I must be one of those cases where something like spontaneous oogenesis (like the virgin Mary) is occurring. After all, my son was born at 230 days gestation (the correct gestation period for a fertilized clone) and he is the only different one. The reason for his difference is because he carries a "Y" gene. If he would have carried two "X" genes then I am certain without a doubt that he would have been identical to my other three children. I am glad that he made a difference in my genetic history; he is the "Y."

After starting to study DNA and genetics, I started noticing similarities between the two fathers. They have similar hand movements, expressions, laughs, voice sounds, etc...I have even sworn that my current husband must be related to me and I am currently tracing the gene lines just to be sure. I have found that we both have Dutch genes and American Indian genes. So, I have learned that people do tend to seek out someone who is more like their own genes.

In order to be healthy and find a healthy relationship with someone, I must first change the unhealthy relationship that I allow my parents to have with me. Allowing such abusiveness and control is actually like a neuropathy. When I allow others to maltreat me over and over, I am actually allowing my neural pathways to become diseased. And as we all know, diseases are hard to overcome, but it can be done. There is hope, however, and I can cure my own neuropathies. We are our own gods and the mind is a powerful tool that we each have. *("Greater is He that is in me than he that is in the world.")* I have been able to break free from the chains that have imprisoned me and altered my DNA for so many years; the jail cell that has imprisoned my mind is no longer locked. Yes, I am still tempted just as an alcoholic is tempted to drink, but I am finally free from my own disease because I know how to overcome it. (My Bible talks a lot about overcoming.) Satan has lost control, and the old adage of "The devil made me do it" is history.

Does anyone ever wonder what kept God up for 6 days? My record is two weeks; I got 2 days of rest then. Again, **Oh, OH** God. I was in love and can remember that feeling. I was awake for 2 weeks straight when I discovered that I was in love with my husband. No drugs, just love. That love abandoned me (God didn't abandon me because "God is love" and I still am here). But I still have the memories and I still take vigilant care of the lovely creations left behind with me. God did leave his lovely creations for us to enjoy on the 8th day. I carry the 8th day with me everywhere I go; that's why I call the 8th day of the week **"SUESS DAY."** Yes, God may have rested on the 7th day, but with **Suess** you get 2 for 1 and you get an extra one; I rested twice as long after two weeks. I really have needed more rest than what I have received, but my Bible states, *"It is better to give than receive."* So, I employ the principle.

I got the extra one when I got two extra chances to do it all over again with my "cloned" girls. God blessed me and gave me another extra one when I conceived my firstborn son. The Bible states that we will be blessed and speaks a lot about "the firstborn son."

I have done so well with regenerating my neural pathways that I now put things where they belong and I cannot find them because I am not looking in the right place. I am so used to looking in the wrong places for misplaced items in which I erroneously placed there that I now place them correctly. It kinda reminds of the saying, "Out with the old and in with the new." It is like untangling a badly tangled wind chime so that it will look pretty and operate as it did when it was fresh out of the box.

I guess you may "get what you pay for." Some people hate change just as much as they hate the fact that the U.S. postage stamp is about to be increased two cents again. Maybe those two cents are not enough. One would think that the USPS has the same prices across the board for the same service. Seems logical, huh? But, not so! I traveled around town hunting a P.O. Box. I wanted a small, letter-size type for $13.00. I finally found one for $19.00 and was told that the individual post offices have different prices. Sometimes you know what to expect and at other times, you can expect the unexpected for sure. I have learned to expect the unexpected. That way, nothing surprises me.

HERITAGE FARMS

GOD WANTS SPIRITUAL FRUIT NOT RELIGIOUS NUTS

Chapter 5: "I" Is For INDIGO

LATE BLOOMERS, EVENTUAL GENIUS': MAKE SENSE

I watched my son as he played with his Barney. It's an interactive Barney. I never really liked Barney, but all my children loved him. My oldest brother, Phil, says Barney's bad because he teaches you to love everybody and that makes you gay. I didn't see anything wrong with being gay 'cause that meant happy. I think he meant homosexual and to him that is a "faux pas." I see "pas" as "sad" and that was sad, eSPECIALly since for 8 years of my life I dated women. Maybe he thought I was "sad" or faux "pas", either way you read it, I saw that he must not like me very much. My dad says, "Some people say it's in the genes and that they are born that way," and disagrees stating to me, "you ought not to hang out with people like that." Yet my whole life, my mom says my dad acted homosexual. So, I ought not to hang out with my dad? What about my siblings: Phil, Tim, and Beth? They have no time for me, so I shouldn't hang out with them either?

My whole life I have been "labeled" and "picked on." I told my mom that I never felt loved and people called me names like "Pinocchio" for my nose. She said, "Well, you told me that, but it's not true." We sometimes believe what others say to us. After all isn't that the associative property? (1+5 = 5+1) Some people say homeschooling is wrong and my kids need

to associate with other kids and be social. Hmm, I have to rethink that one because if I associate with the other 5 then I may turn out just like them. I don't want to be prejudicial; I want to be judicial, like justice. I want us all to be "just us." I still accept them all, but I know they don't accept me. I still have time for them and if I am busy, I call back. They have no time for me and it seems they only call for me to have time for them; then, off they go again. Kinda like hi-ho, hi-ho.
My mother started to name me Snow White. Now I see why. It's a bad feeling to be a-lone in this world, but then again we are each born alone and we each die alone. That's the only time we need to be alone. The rest of the time we need to be with each other. That's the time to be social; no wonder the Bible reads, "When two or more are gathered, I am there." Some say people have magnetic personalities. That must be me because I am attracted to a lot of people, but I must be bi-polar because when it comes to my family the polarity switches and they have an aversion to me. I must have the lowest IQ in the family, I thought perhaps even "1", but being alone, being a/one must mean that I am the smartest one in the family. A/one = Together, and sometimes I feel they are out **to**-**get**-**her** and all together. Again you get 2 for 1 there. I always learned that home is where the heart is and that's true; my "**HART**" is here at home. Something's left out, I know. But my Hart is my baby. He was singled out because he had extra "2 1". First he has "extras" and that makes him "*mentally retarded*" according to the doctors, then he's my baby and that makes him a "1" in my book. He's just that, <u>**the only one**</u>. I say that's intelligent and the doctor's are stupid.

My computer's "Seuss Cat in The Hat" screensaver appears when our computer has been idle for a while and the Seuss music comes on. We get up and either hit the mute, move the mouse, or type a key; the screen goes back again. Twice since I have been writing, the screensaver has come on. Twice my son quit playing with his Barney and went over to the computer and moved the mouse, and the other time he typed a key. My son just turned two years old. He is supposed to be "stupid" or "mentally retarded" or something, but he knew that annoyed me, and he quit what he was doing for me. (Sounded loving to me.) After all, love isn't love until you give it away. And God is love. I think love reflects love always. Love is the only thing that reflects itself. Sometimes you see <u>lone</u> depending on how you reflect it, but love never reflects hate. So if he loved me then he got it from me. He took time for me because I took time for him. I must be in that stupid crowd because I keep spending time on other people who don't have time for me, or does that make me smarter than them? That's in the < = > signs. We are supposed to love God because he first loved us. But if God is in us all that means we all have love. How come some people don't give it out? Is therefore love > hate? Looks like "pac-man," huh? Hate just keeps eating up all that love.

I saw a bumper Sticker once that read, **"To love or to kill a child should be an easy choice."** I now agree. Plain and unvarnished is the truth, and the truth shall set you free indeed.

Are they called "late bloomers" or "eventual genius'"? For whatever the reason, my children-each and every one-have a different design in their wiring than most, making their neural pathways different in the ways that they learn and perceive the world around them; although, I think this attribute makes them quite more attractive to other people. I believe that being different in your own way and making a difference in the world is more attractive than being the same as everyone else.

By laws of nature, my husband and I carry these same genes that we have passed on to our children. What a unique gift from God that we have been given. The only difference between my daughters and my son is that the doctor's stole that precious gift of "perfectness" and "togetherness" from me with my son. It's a crying shame that doctors are not held accountable for "classifying" the intelligence of babies based on a look or a chromosome count. Delving into the protected genetic identity of an individual rips the pride, integrity, and personal identity from that person. No one has the right to "classify" someone as an "idiot" because of a particular physical look or because of a particular chromosome in his or her genetic makeup. We were all created in the image of God, and not only does God not make mistakes, but I also don't believe God was an idiot.

My experience is that there are different ways of learning in us all. Visual, auditory, and kinesthetic learning styles are some of the ways that individuals learn. Some people have a combination of two or more learning styles, and there are some of us that are very fortunate to have expanded into new and different ways of learning by enhancing or developing new neural pathways. We each grow and develop in our own way and at our own customized rate. We all have disabilities and we all have abilities; likewise, some will have the ability to read this book and understand every single word and why it is written the way that it is. Others will be totally lost and their brain will immediately "classify" me as "stupid" or "crazy." Depending on the ways you have been taught to learn, the ways you have been treated by others, and the ways you were loved or unloved as well as the perceptions you have of such will determine what neural pathways are developed and encouraged; these in turn have a major impact on who you become as an individual. This reminds me of the study that was done years ago in which children were greatly affected by the way they were treated by the teachers that were given information contrary to the actual picture of the student. The teachers reflected to the students what they were told by other people. Subsequently, the students were treated in accordance with how someone told them they were even though the opposite was in fact true. The study was never repeated because of the detrimental effects that it had on so many lives.

Speaking and interacting with my 95 year old grandmother, I have learned that repeated and ingrained neural pathways are near impossible to change because of their deep roots; however, new neural pathways can always be generated using the perceptions of the old traditions. The older we get the more inherent we become; hence the phrase "you cannot teach an old dog new tricks." The phrase should read, "You can't teach an old dog to change his old ways, but you can create new ways to cope with the old tricks." Having said this, you can see how you generate new "neural pathways" in order to cope with the old way of doing things. This frequently takes much talent, innovation, and repetition. Once you change the traditional ways of doing your routine, you change your neural pathways and/or create new ones. For instance, if you intensely dislike cantaloupe and you start eating it every morning for breakfast, a new neural pathway will form in the brain.

Neural pathways can be difficult to change once they have developed into unfavorable habits; it is much easier to create a new pathway by experiencing new ideas, innovative concepts, and different ways of doing things. Exposure to different cultures is a fantastic way to create a new neural pathway, for example. I have also found other relatively inexpensive ways to develop neural pathways in yourself and especially your baby if you are already a computer owner. Computers come preinstalled with a "Windows Media Player" that features a variety of "visualizations" that will accompany any music CD that is installed. Even if you are limited in your senses, it is a fantastic tool. I have found that with children, a CD that has their name in every song is more useful in stimulating and developing neural pathways. The key here is to stimulate as many of the senses as possible at the same time.

The key to becoming a well-rounded person is through developing your 9 senses. Traditionally speaking, most of us have been trained that there are only 5 senses: sight, smell, touch, taste, and hearing. However, there are 4 "non-traditional" senses recognized by scientists that have been forgotten: precognition, clairvoyance, telepathy, and empathy. Because many people have not developed these "bonus" senses, they disregard their existence.

I want to say this to you, you, and YOU,
I wish for no one like YOU to say who.
Please let it be known, please go and share,
That a girl named Suess
is someone who cares.
I want you to matter, yes even you,

Red, white, and black, yes yellow and BLUE.
I'll end this book with
one phrase that fits all;
A person's a person no matter how small!

Three of my children: Star, Charlie Hart, and Maze at a Seussical rehearsal.

"V" IS FOR VIOLET

Colorful Collection
Of Pictures & Poems

This is a picture from my daughter Maze. It looks better in color.

One By One, I'll Love You So

Trickum Road came falling down
Falling Down, Falling Down
Trickum Road came falling down
My good baby.
Take the house and set them free
Set them free, set them free
Take the house and set them free
My good baby.
How will she bring them up?
Bring them up, Bring them up
How will she bring them up?
My good baby.
Bring them up with love & grace
Love & Grace, Love & Grace
Bring them up with love & grace
My good baby.

Love & Grace I have some
I have some, I have some
Love & Grace I have some
My good baby.
Bring them up one by one
One by One, One by One
Bring them up one by one
My good baby.
One by one, I'll love you so
Love you so, love you so
One by One I'll love you so
My good baby.

Thank you God for all four of my wonderful children and all their "21" chromosomes; thank you Lord for all the extras in their 23 chromosomes as well. Thank you God for being right.

Universal Poem From I

I do not want it changed a bit
Lest you see me have a fit

I wanted it printed as it is
Suess says do this for the kids.

It must be printed just like this;
For to the world, it is my kiss.

I want everyone just like you
To never forget the color blue.

Suess Loves The Little Children

Red & Yellow, Black & White
All of you are out of sight.
Don't forget there is a blue
It might be me, or it may have been you.
You are special; I wish we met.
You are different; please don't forget.
Let no one ever, ever tell you–
"You are stupid, 'cuz you are YOU."

An Ultrasound picture of my son at two weeks gestation after falling down a flight of stairs—the picture features a side view of what appears to be an angel praying over my uterus. No medical explanation or any other explanation can be found for this occurrence. The angel was noticed after I prayed for God to send me a sign or an angel that everything would be ok.

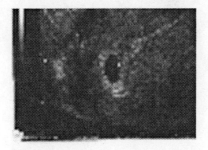

Here I Am

Here I am, it's just me
Here I am, can't you see
Here I am, I'm not you
Here I am, I AM SUESS.

Here I am, here I come
It's just me: I am someone.

I may not do it quite like him
I may not do it quite like her
I may not do it quite like you
But I know I do it quite like SUESS.

I may not see it just like him
I may not see it just like her
I may not see it just like you
But I know I see it just like SUESS.

I may not learn at all like him
I may not learn at all like her
I may not learn it all like you
But I know I learn it all like SUESS.

I may not look just like her
I may not look just like him
I may not look just like you
But I do know I look just like SUESS.

I may have extras, extra genes
I may have less, if you know what I mean.
I may have added chromosomes
I may have less, but I still have some.

I may have talent; I might have some
I may have sense; I might have none.
I know there's one thing, I know for sure
There is something, there is a cure.

A cure for you, a cure for me
A gift of love, can't you see?
Look around at all the signs
See us all, all the kinds.
So here I come, here I am
Sometimes I like blue eggs & ham

This "Y' is a natural occurrence in the center of the tree trunk in the Champion's backyard.

I Don't Wanna Be Somebody New

I don't wanna be somebody new
I don't wanna be just like you.
I like being just like me.
Really that's all I wanna be.

God made me to be different than you.
He didn't make me because he didn't like you.
He made me to be different, like you.
He made me just to accompany you.

He was pleased with your birth.
As He was pleased with all earth.
He created A'dam imaging Himself.
He wanted Eve to be a big help.

Who ever would've thought
You would get two for one
"Cause God created A'dam
And He wasn't quite done.

Man didn't need to talk all alone
That's why woman wasn't a clone.
Some people think and when they do,
They don't even think there may be a **YOU**.

I don't wanna be somebody new
I don't wanna be just like you.
I wanna be just who I am.
I wanna eat blue eggs 'n ham.

AS SUESS WAS GOING TO ST. IVES

As I was going to ST. IVES,
I met so many with different lives.
Many people, Many children, Many ways.
I'VE heard a lot, seen so much, and heard them say:
"Children should be seen and not be heard,"
WaS ONE phrase I thought absurd.

I know eaCH child SHould have a voice,
I know eaCH child SHould have a Choice.
A HeART Shouldn't be judged,
but LOVEd so much;
A HeART Should be LOVEd,
HEld and SUCH.

I C "professionals"
NOW walking in "OZ."
I am saying THIS ALL
JuST beCaUSe,
I do Hope one day
U ALL CAN reTURN
2 the fabUlous lAND
E. PLURIBUS UNUM.

E. Pluribus Unum
On all our money
Do you know what
It really means honey?

The Phrase is Latin, now I am done.
It really means "Out of many, One."

We're All The Same With Different Names

We are all God's Children
We are all the same
We each are different
We each have a name.

Doesn't matter if it's Black or White
Doesn't matter if it's yours or mine
What matters most is your sight
To see us all as one kind.

Can we talk about me?
Oh, can't you see?
We talk about U Usually.

I wanna talk about I
I wanna talk about me
Can't we talk about us together?
You & Me.

National Make A Difference Day

October 22nd,
Today is the day,
To make a difference in what U say.
Make sure U match
what U say & do,
Remember U R making
a statement of you.

I do not like it,
not one bit!
That some of you
just sit & sit.
When U know & see
there is a need,
U should be brethren,
a friend in deed.

When U see someone
who's in distress
Take a look at U

and reassess.
R U one of those
who waits & sits?
I C some of you
are just hypocrites.

So if U think
U R on a vacation,
To me, I think
U R an Irritation.
If U R one of those
who does NADA
Remember me when
U R in Camp Grenada.

Do not call me
to say hello
Don't call me
when I have to go.
Don't look me up
when I have fame,
Know me now,
I have a name.

Fairground ST NE
50 →

EXIT ONLY
← ENTRANCES →

A FINAL NOTE about the author: "B" IS FOR BLUE

I have discovered that sometimes caring for other people is offensive. I believe God is the center of the universe and some people are convinced that they themselves are in fact the center of our universe instead. I've seen some people who own multiple pairs of the same exact kind of reading glasses; you know the kind that you buy at the corner drug store. I asked why so many pairs seeing as one can wear but only one pair at a time. Odd, but with all those reading glasses, some people still can't see a thing at all with any of the pairs of glasses that they have. Others can see clearly without any glasses at all.

When some people think, they fail to convey or express their thoughts with others so as to conclude or come up with a joint effort in completing a project, especially when the eventual outcome concerns all involved parties. A meeting of the minds is an essential ingredient in every relationship that coexists. If we as human beings don't meet in the middle, then we shouldn't bother meeting at all because I don't know the path back to your place and you are obviously lost without my road map. An example of how lost one would be in this situation is if I gave you only my route on a map to you and you were leading me blindly with what you thought to be a true and correct picture of the path on which you need to embark. Some people really don't need to use maps to find their way because they have an impeccable sense of direction. I may not always be aware of the direction that I initially am traveling but make no mistake that I am very alert as to where I have been prior to that moment.

I do hope that my children have at least started to learn one of life's very important lessons—an invaluable self-help tool that has taken me almost a full 40 years, 4 children, and 1 cremated soul to realize—a multi-faceted lesson embracing the following concepts:

1. The money ain't worth two cents, and sometimes the "love" isn't either.
2. Self-worth is dignified by not allowing others to control your way(s) of thinking.
3. Let <u>no one</u> compromise your value(s).

4. Control only has the power you allow it to have.
5. Stand up for yourself even when the world fails you; forgiveness in due time only emanates from a strong personality and a reliable memory.
6. Always remember one is most vulnerable to submission of being controlled and manipulated by others when one is visibly helpless and at her highest time of need.
7. Never allow yourself to be completely dependent on someone else because once discovered, you have opened your soul to be destroyed by the words of other people's mouths. Senseless babble becomes ingrained into a self-realization that destroys ones self-worth, self-esteem, and dignity.

The neural pathways created in your brain as a result lead to a vicious cycle of abuse and emotional trauma that virtually never fails. The cycle becomes like a revolving door with no exit. In these situations, one falls victim to the beliefs of others and one loses his/her personal points of view. One's worth becomes shaped into an inflexible mold that is formed solely on what others profess you to be. Your opinion now lacks sustenance as you become weaker; whereas, strength even in a sole number becomes unattainable. Negativity becomes your only reality. It becomes easier to "go with the flow" of agonizing control and submission to the choking and drowning efforts of quicksand. This becomes the most comfortable option replacing the comfort zone of having your own personal belief system, which may or may not be the same as someone else's belief system. Personal happiness becomes dependent on making others happy. The moral and myth becomes such that one will suffer tremendously & willingly, and one will even compromise their own feelings just to suffice others. Submission into modern day slavery becomes self-inflicted. The wounds become larger and harder to heal and eventually the wounds become infected. Self-actualization becomes an unfortunate cancer as good nourishing cells turn rancid like sour milk; the bacteria multiplies ever so quickly and takes over. Neural pathways become damaged to the point of near impossibility to regenerate and building new neural pathways is dimmed by the destruction of **you** by others. The wiring diagram in your brain becomes so entangled and in such a mess that little room is left for normality. You allow yourself to become convinced that change is bad and that you deserve no better; reality is change is good, and you deserve only the best.

I wanted to end my book with at least one positive quality to say about the "other people" in my life. This chapter is both easy and difficult for me to include in this book. It is easy in that I tend to always observe people for the better qualities even though they mistreat me. Forgiving seems to be one of my healthier qualities that I possess. Although forgiving others is not the same as forgetting, I try not to remember and that is how I get by in my life. Consequently, my entire life I have been "preached to" about how the Bible says you are supposed to forgive. Most of the ones giving me this advice are the very ones that I feel have done me wrong. I never quite understood that one. Left and right and all around, I am expected to continuously forgive (and in their minds that includes "forget.") the way that I have been used and abused by others. One might argue that I allowed myself to get into these situations; yes and no. First, God allowed me to be born. So, is it His fault also? Christians do not typically believe that we "chose" our parents and Christians believe that God has a plan for our life before we are even "knitted together in our mother's womb." God did a wonderful thing allowing me to be born; for without me, I never would have had 4 precious children to love and give life to. **God is love.**

My mother was born Mary Joyce Fielder on March 24, 1933 and later became a White and then she became a Bramlett. She is one of the best Mathematicians that I have ever known. She is a fine Math Instructor and a shrewd businesswoman. After remarrying Kenneth Earl Bramlett, she later became divorced and he subsequently died about a year later in December 2004. She gave birth to me on November 11, 1965.

My father was born Aubrey Hoyt White on October 8, 1930. He is one of the best brick masons I know and he constructed many of the houses in the neighborhood in which I now live. Raising orchids used to be a favorite pastime and he was president of the Atlanta Orchid Society for many years. After my parents divorced when I turned 18 years old, he remarried someone named Jan Harrison (who I never met); I heard she died of cancer. He later married a fine woman named Vivian who is a retired RN. I always liked her and she has had many long conversations on the phone with me and never once complained about "minutes." She seemed to always have time for me and she talked to me for hours on end sometimes on the phone.

My oldest brother was born Phillip Anthony White on January 21, 1952. Being very "intelligent," he used to build satellites that are put into space. Subsequently, he worked for a local telephone company, Bellsouth, despite how much he had previously disliked the company. He now runs a small private school in Augusta, Georgia. His first marriage to Janet Sue Crowe (Angel) ended with her death while he served in the USAF. For a hobby, he builds ultralight airplanes. His failed second marriage to Dotty Poehnelt resulted in the birth of identical triplet girls (Rebecca Lynn, Barbara Joanne, and Laura Leigh) followed by another girl (Christina Marie) 13 months later. Becky, Bobbi, and Laura have graduated high school and currently either hold at least one job if not two and/or go to college; they have done quite well with being self-supportive. Christina married a man who worked for Motorola named Song Chung whom she dated throughout high school. She went to college and earned a degree in teaching in which she utilized for a short time to teach others. They currently have one son, Jonathan. Currently, Phil is married to a charming woman named Rhonda who has fraternal twins, Cayla and Caleb, who are about to finish high school.

Next in line is my brother, Aubrey Timothy White, who was born on October 27th, 1954. He is an expert on fishing and currently works for the USPS. He travels around the country as a professional speaker for companies that promote fishing equipment. He has co-authored a book about fishing. For him, 4th times a charm. He is currently married to a quiet woman named Vicki; they have one precious son Alexander Nicholas who is currently in high school.

My sister Elizabeth Anne White Case lives in Lake Mary, Florida with her precious daughter Mikaela. Beth was born September 8, 1960. A bank currently employs her. She takes a strong interest in her child and always has her involved in activities outside of school education. Never married to the loser Michael Case who avoided the support of their child for years, she has managed to provide a home, an education as well as nice clothes for Mikaela. Mikaela is an excellent flute player.

I was born Susan Dorothy White 40 years ago. My failed marriage to Randy Milam resulted in no children. My firstborn Karla Michelle Hand was born by cesarean section on November 21, 1986 to Mark Jonathan Hand and myself. Her dad turned 50 years old this year and he currently resides in Jackson, Georgia. Michelle currently is a training manager at the local Taco Bell; she is self-supportive and currently lives on her own with a roommate. She graduated high school with a college prep diploma and a two-year technical diploma in which she took Law Enforcement classes. Karla Michelle speaks Spanish fluently as a second language, and she at present is interested in learning the Japanese language. Currently she is entertaining the notion of becoming an attorney. She hopes to move to Canada with her boyfriend Anthony.

Presently, I am a dedicated mom and loving devoted wife to my current husband, Charles Edward TenEyck, Jr., who was born March 27, 1960. He is one of the best-known auto body technicians and mechanics in this town. He fathered two children, Angel & Crystal, before me by another wife. They currently live in Ohio and Crystal (his second born) recently had a son. We married on December 2, 2000 and we currently have three home birthed children together. Our first child, Mazur Gemini was born on March 14, 1997. She currently is in the 3rd grade and is presently home schooled. She loves to play with her friends in the neighborhood and is an excellent sister to her siblings. She favors unicorns and her favorite color used to be orange ☺ She currently likes the color blue. She enjoys swimming even though we do not get a chance to do very much of it due to lack of a pool facility. Maze likes to collect music boxes. She enjoys going to the park with her younger sister, Charlese Star who was born on August 10, 1998. Star is in the 2nd grade and also home schooled. She enjoys playing with her friends and also likes to swim. Her and her sister spent 3 years learning to dance tap and ballet at Rhythm Dance Center. Changing interests as well as money constraints caused them both to take other interests. The girls are often referred to as twins because of their identical looks. (Coincidentally, my daughter Karla Michelle favors them in that her childhood pictures look the same as theirs in many photos.) Both Star and Maze enjoy pizza but Star prefers to be a vegetarian like her older sister Karla. Star never liked meat from birth. (And they say you cannot be born vegetarian because that's a choice.) Star favors rainbows but prefers the color purple and she collects teapots and crosses. Both girls enjoy "walking the mall" and riding on the merry-go-round at NorthPoint Mall in Alpharetta, Georgia. They are all proud of their only brother "Charlie Hart" who was born at 230 days gestation on July 20, 2003. (To my surprise that is the same gestational period as for a fertilized clone.) C.H. enjoys music and fights for shared time at the computer. He enjoys the water like his sisters and loves to watch T.V. Being very intelligent, he responds to 5 different languages currently. He is a scrapper and wants to be included in everything. He enjoys "dance time" with the radio. He loves to learn and his favorite toy is Barney. He is a real "charmer" and very independent. Like all of my children, he is stubborn and his behavior reflects such. Although my children are well behaved because of my excellent parenting, they act up more than their fair share sometimes. I join in sometimes just to make it even. My children are very perceptive and know the meaning of true love. Understanding that talk is cheap and money can't but you love, they are very giving children.

Faced with a foreclosure sale on our home (where they were born and raised) today, my 3 minor children have bound together with me in a time of sadness. With the exception of one man, Mohammed, who assisted me one night, no one has helped us move our belongings out of our house until recently after our house sold; it was then when my husband returned briefly to assist me, and my father and step-mother Vivian came to help us briefly. (My father has the exact record of how long he was there.) Michael and Bernie also helped from time to time, as did Aimee. Most of the moving was done by yours truly. We all feared that we were going to lose our personal belongings just as we lost our home. Maze was found crying in bed last night and did not want to leave our home of 10 years; after all, she was born here. As I held her tightly, I let her know that I was scared as well and that everything will change for the better as long as we stand together as a family. I decided to include a few notes about what I personally think. Here it is:

About people: There are 3 kinds of people in this world: those who make things happen; those who watch things happen; and those who wonder what the hell happened. I always taught my children about feelings and humanity. One should not judge a book by its cover and everyone has more than one book to be read. I believe that we are a reflection of society and that if you do not stand for something, then you will fall for anything. I stand for justice and equal rights for all abilities and think people should be treated fairly despite their race, religion, personal beliefs, sexual preference, age or gender. We all know that hind sight is 20/20 but a lot of people prefer not to use that peripheral vision because they are accustomed to tunnel vision. Narrowing of the vision causes blindness.

About religion: I believe the family should be the center of the church and I believe religion is a personal choice and a fundamental right by God. Organized religion does not really appeal to me because some churches will only assist you if you are a member of their parish or live in their county. All the while you can be raised in a church and can get assistance neither with your place to live, nor support in court when your child has received counseling from the church and you ask for a letter of reference to such. Additionally, I think Joel and Victoria Osteen have a wonderful ministry at Lakewood Church in Houston, Texas and around the world.

About government: My belief is that there are too many people in this world wrapped up in labels and there is an abuse of power in many facets of government. The people in government should be better trained to do simple tasks like phone transfers, and government and public service employees should know and understand what each facet of government does. In addition, they should have an updated list of phone numbers for all departments. Police officers should be better trained and should carry an updated codebook at all times. Also, it should not take 3 police cars for backup on an unruly juvenile when their measures have failed in the past.

About Public Education: My confidence in public schooling has declined due to the labels that are imposed on our children and the current practices of pointing out obesity in children; children are not learning what they should be learning in kindergarten. While on the subject of "free public schooling," I believe that the State misrepresents offering a free education to every child in this country. I spent more money just in the first month after enrolling my children in public school than I spent in an entire year of home schooling. I believe that Cobb County (as well as other counties) employees with the board of education need to be informed that we as citizens do pay their salaries and they do work for us. (Carol Durand with the Cobb Board of Ed. stated to me that she was "too busy helping hurricane victims to answer my questions," and that "she did not work for me and I did not pay her salary.") I think that every class deserves a mandated 'teacher's helper' and that assistants should not be limited to 'special ed' and 'kindergarten.'

About the Lottery: Instead of paying out millions of dollars to a single winner on the lottery, I firmly believe that the governor should delegate a million or two providing needed school supplies, which include a personal laptop computer to every child K-12. In addition, I think that property owners should have their taxes reduced or offset for school taxes when they do not have children that attend a public school. Additionally, when there is an excess in lottery monies, the excessive amounts should be given towards educational taxes and funding for our schools to educate our youth.

About school lunches: My neighbor Doris told me that her grandson takes $5.00 a day to school for lunch. She stated he liked the pizza and it was **$2.50 per slice.** Funny, because I thought school lunches were federally subsidized and were supposed to be less expensive or at least "reasonable." Isn't it even more peculiar that I can purchase 3 Domino's pizzas for $5.00 each? One can even eat at an "all-you-can-eat pizza buffet" for $3.29. I cannot afford the school lunches and the choices are limited for lunch menu selection either way. I like to monitor and control what my children eat as they help to make choices in their menu selection based on what we have and their personal eating habits. Having been infuriated in the past by employees of the public school system defaming my child & other children in front of other children about what they bring for a snack and/or a lunch, I embarked on that battle once more when Maze told me that she "was allowed to finish her cinnamon roll this time" but "couldn't bring it any more." Upon notification and conference with the assistant principal and principal of my daughter's school, I took a stand and informed the school that I was her parent and that they had no right whatsoever deciding what my children eat. When confronted with the remark that "sugar makes everyone hyper" and "chocolate was not a nutritious snack," I voiced my opinion based on knowledgeable research and informed them that they cannot group people all into one category (like math teaches us), and that sugar does not make me or my children hyper. I do think parents should have authority over what they send their child to eat. I then believe it is up to the child to refuse or accept choices they had a part in making. I continued as I told them that chocolate bread was a famous customary snack for French children and that research had been done on chocolate to show that it contains flavinoids, which are beneficial, and that chocolate has been found to improve memory.

About Parenting and Having Sex: Love has everything to do with mating. Unless you are devoted to caring for another person until you death do you part, do not engage in behavior that may result in having a baby.

Children will always be just that and parenting doesn't begin at birth; parenting begins before conception. Parenting does not end at 18; that age is when your "test results" come in and you can self-evaluate. As a parent, you have numerous chances along the way to "check your answers and correct them" before you receive your score. When you realize you have failed, the Great Instructor gives you ample opportunity to correct your mistake. You may argue with the result and state that you have the correct answer but the answers are very clear with the writing always on the wall.

About doctors and hospitals: I think doctors charge too much for their expertise and I only utilize doctors if I need a prescription or I want a certain test or procedure that requires a doctor's order. I believe that hospitals should not employ medical personnel that violate moral code of ethics and state law. I believe a lot of disease and illness is iatrogenically caused and that a majority of the time unnecessary tests are charged to a patient solely for the purpose of obtaining money. I believe that patient rights are not respected and that doctors and nurses as well as other medical personnel that do not give informed consent and respect others rights should be suspended until they have a working knowledge of such.

About attorneys: My belief here is that if you are not familiar with the law then don't ask me. If you have to ask me what law or case that I am referencing, then you need to go back to law school and retake the state boards exam. Everyone cannot know everything, but the smart person looks up the answer. Attorneys should clarify what information is presented to them and also they should investigate the case that is being presented to them. Lawyers should not limit themselves and should have higher aspirations of upholding the law both civilly and criminally.

About friends: Don't expect people to treat you any differently than what you expect to treat them. If you have had someone treat you better than what you think you have treated him or her, then consider it a blessing and thank God; don't forget to thank that friend as well. Thanking people for acts of kindness is not only respectful and proper but it shows how much you appreciate their friendship.

About Bibles: Everyone should live by one. My personal choice is the Holy Bible. I believe people should not only practice what they preach, but also they should live by the Bible that they carry. So many times people mistakenly believe that "appearing at a church every time the doors are open (or at least every Sunday) with bible in hand" qualifies them as a bonafide Christian obeying God's word; they also portray that their ticket to heaven is the same. For someone to exclaim to me that believing that Jesus died on the cross for our sins and He is the Son of God, and that is what gets your soul to heaven is only part of the truth. Truth be known, one must have a deeper understanding of that proverbial statement so as to understand exactly who Jesus was. I photographed a sign once that read, "Jesus modeled service. John 13:5-15." I found that sign posted outside Sandy Plains Baptist Church in Marietta, Georgia. That church has helped my children and I with food several times and I have personally met the pastor and believe he is a fine gentleman from what I know of him. Additionally, I asked that church to pray for us and they sent a lovely note to me in the mail denoting the fact that they remembered to say a special prayer for me. No one knows how that small token of kindness made my rainy day turn into sunshine. A big thank you goes out to Sandy Plains Baptist Church. My current belief is they practice what they preach. As for the rest of the "Christian world" as well as "the Christians" in my family, I believe that reading, understanding, and implementing I John in the Bible will give you a better perception of what it means to believe that Jesus is the Son of God. That book of the Bible may be where **You** find your one-way ticket to a better place.

He has the whole world in His hands and no one is superior to another. I do not like the standard version of <u>Jesus Loves the Little Children of the World</u> song because the song leaves out the "blue babies." Without blue, all the colors of the rainbow are not there and it takes all kinds. People really should practice what they preach. And if you do not like the way I am living or you do not understand my viewpoint, then come over to my side and find out what you have been missing: meanwhile you can show me what I have been missing.

Very Truly and Sincerely Yours,

A girl named SUESS

P.S. When you think you have been wronged, try to inform the person how you feel first to see if you can remedy the situation. When all efforts fail to correct the wrong, tell the world until someone listens. When you have realized that you have been wrong (as we all are wrong sometimes) admit it, change it, and right the wrong. And that's my 2 cents.

F.Y.I.

On certain U.S. coins, the letter "V" is used in the spelling of the word "TRUST". The letters "U" and "V" were used interchangeably in medieval times. Until about 1800, these two letters were not given separate alphabetical listings. In the recent ages, many sculptors have used the "V" in place of the "U". Mostly for artistic purposes, the "V" is used in place of the "U" to represent the permanence and long-time significance of the artists' work. Designing artists may choose to spell "TRUST" with a "V" as is in all the Peace Dollar coins. The U.S. mint manufactured more than 190 million $1 coins of this type from 1921 through 1935. The letter "V" is sometimes used in place of the letter "U" in wording on public buildings as well.

As far as that subdivision "STONEHURST" is concerned, "ST" "UR" "HURT ONE." I know I see "Her ONE SUESS" right in the middle. That is where I find "SUESS" in "STONEHURST" and "left" hanging on reflectively, "HEY SUESS", and there my friend is your **"Y"**.

"Children should be seen and not heard" and "Let your food stop your mouth" are phrases my father often recited. To me, he is a "Hush Husher" with the sole intent of gaining control over his target.
He turns a deaf ear to the Bible verses that apply to him.
Raising children just doesn't end at conception, birth, or when one turns 18 or moves out of the house. My father swears by recent statement to me that I "have been conning (him) for 22 years." God, please tell me how I have been conning him, and what the hell he is referencing because surely I do not know. He must be referring to joining my lawsuit against a place that used to exist named Straight Inc. He said he joined my lawsuit only for "moral support" but demanded half of my out-of-court settlement because of his "failed marriage" and inability to "go to Hawaii" while he and my mother had me imprisoned there for 11 months for **NO REASON** other than to control me and keep me at home when I turned 18. When you agree or consent to having a baby, you have made a lifetime commitment to another person. My parents never knew or learned that (even though they probably will proclaim so), but they are mighty "showy" and I think they may even believe that their belief system is correct. I told my mother once that my husband was choking me with a vacuum cleaner cord and she proclaimed, "I want to know how the children's first day of school went," ignoring my comment. My children and I are a package deal. What's worse is I once told her, "All I really need is a hug from my mother right now." Her reply, **"I can't." Those two hurtful words will stick in my brain until the day that my physical body leaves this earth and I die.**

Whereas, "people who do really need the services are hurried along out the door because they don't want to deal with them," Karen White added. The medical file I finally received read that Cobb DFCS had all intentions of adopting out my son and also read that I knew he wasn't coming home. I personally think that someone needs to be sued for all the pain caused to my family and I. My children were even told by WellStar personnel in my presence that they were not allowed to come and see their brother because we elect not to put poisonous vaccines in our children. What difference did it make if I came unvaccinated or if they came unvaccinated? I know the difference: abuse of power, control, stupidity, and harassment. The sole purpose of their actions in my opinion and in the opinion of the people who know my entire story was to take my son, make an example of me for having chose a homebirth, and to cover their own ass for mistakes they made in not following the law. It really pangs me to see other people trying to control others medical/religious choices. Also, I know it is a crime not to give informed consent. Very few people know what that really entails. Informed consent means, "Given all the possible known scenarios and outcomes of a particular situation, or in this case medical treatment, a person then has the right to choose or decline the procedure." I see so many ignoring peoples' rights these days. Additionally, I see so many forgetting that we are ALL humans and we ALL have rights. We ALL have a voice to ultimately be heard rather than just seen.

I had told her that I wanted to go but I could not find anyone then to go with me. Everyone had "more important things to do." I will never forget the look on her face when she said, "I have 10 reserved V.I.P. seats and I have been looking for the 10th person to go with me. (She only had 9 committed to go.) You are the 10th person!" Tears begin to roll down my face as I learned that she personally knew Joel since he was a child and she knew his father, John Osteen. My mother had said she would come with me this year but I never heard from her and she was a "No Show". That is typical for her. I had an extra ticket because no one else would come with me either, not even my husband. Lakewood Church had so graciously provided me with tickets because I could not afford them.

My late Great Aunt Helen frequently stopped at Lakewood Church on her way to Mexico to build churches. As a matter of fact, I was supposed to go with her on her next trip, but her next trip was to heaven. I was devastated seeing as NOT ONE SOUL CAME TO MY HOUSE TO LET ME KNOW SHE HAD DIED, and I have an aunt who attended the funeral; she lives 6 miles away from me. My aunt is the one who is married to the man whom everyone in my family professes does not like children; however, he sits on the Board of Directors for the Cobb County Department of Family & Children Services. Maybe that's why they "harass good parents that don't need their services," stated to me directly by Karen White, 'social worker' for Cobb County. She identified the judge as "stedman" and the court appointed attorney as "harris" without even "reading the file" as **she** expressed it. She also stated, "they tend to harass people who don't need services from DFCS."

He also knew that "it takes all kinds" and that some of creation would inevitably just provide "lip service" (termed well by Honorable Judge Irma Glover). In addition He knew that we all would have our unique and individual abilities that would be favorable to some and unfavorable to others. He stated he wanted to "provide man with a help or companion" and that He knew that "animals' could not provide such. Everyone cannot have the same companion, so as a result of Adam & Eve's sin He cast them out of the Garden of Eden and commanded them to be fruitful and multiply. Merciful indeed is our God because He knew that children would also bring us much JOY. I think that's why you must "become as a child to enter the kingdom of heaven." Repeatedly the Bible refers to "the least of these."

Joel Osteen mentioned that in his sermon at Phillip's Arena in Atlanta, Georgia Friday night. That preacher ALWAYS seems to be speaking directly to me. I was so sure that someone had called him on my behalf and asked him to pray for me because during his closing prayer, EVERY WORD applied to me. He spoke of bad childhoods; being mistreated by spouse, family, and friends; bad financial situations; losing your home; and people like your spouse saying you are worthless and cursing you. He inspires me and I am trying to follow his principles. He said to give my burdens to God and trust in Him; he has helped me choose to stay living just one more day. I was sitting 6th row back, dead center. Last year, I was on the 3rd row behind Victoria Osteen; I like her because she has conviction. When she speaks, she does so with conviction. My late Aunt Helen Mann was the precious responsible party for inviting me then.

That ought to be illegal to post such signs and not heed to that very protocol. Of course, not an attorney anywhere seems to have the time or the knowledge to see such violations. I wonder what do those attorneys learn in Law School; maybe I should say, "What do they forget." I may learn the true answer to that question soon because my 18-year-old has mentioned going to Law School to become a lawyer. She is very argumentative and defiant; I know she would be an excellent lawyer, civil or criminal or otherwise.

I took a break from packing just to jot these notes down and I decided to go outside and exercise my right of standing on the sidewalk and looking at the "sign that God sent" in my yard. It is an intersection crossing sign that reads," SIMS Dr." and I do so like to view it because of the way I now read. I see "Im Dr. Susi" and I also read, "Si Im Dr.SDW." SD stands for Susan Dorothy White, my maiden name.

I have seen a different "viewpoint" since the birth of my son and I am unaware whether or not it is related to a tumor or some other "labeled" medical condition. Whatever the reason, I am happy for it because I have been able to help others understand and appreciate all the differences in our DNA and all the relativity to one true God. I have sought the true meaning of the words within the covers of the HOLY BIBLE (all versions). I learned that in Genesis where God said," to be fruitful and multiply," there was a reason. He truly is an omniscient, omnipotent God; for He knew even when A'dam was created in His image that the DNA proteins would regroup and form new creations.

Persons in these groups know exactly who they are and which groups they are in usually; however, many are still in that denial phase. I am aware that there are quite a few other groups that can be stereotyped without question.

No one can ever begin to imagine how I felt when I overheard "WellStar Kennestone Hospital personnel-nurses and doctors" refer to my child as "THE DOWN'S CHILD." Being on the inside of a drawn curtain when I nursed my baby, my rocker backed up to the station where doctors would record daily notes on the computer. Some of the "unethical" conversation about documentation I overheard was such: "you cannot write 'seizures,' you have to write 'seizure like activity.'" I now know after reviewing my son's medical file that this damned hospital was fabricating lies to justify their behavior and iatrogenically caused illness. They even wrote a letter in return to me when I questioned all their "medical malpractice" and "abuse of power" that stated they did not even report all of the CT Scans that they performed on my son to the insurance company. Doing so would have clearly sent 'red flags' flying everywhere and probably it would have caused an investigation into the "Y's" and scope of their practice. Bear in mind that all of these "non-stabilizing procedures" were performed without express consent from me, my husband, or anyone else for that matter.

Take into consideration that they clearly post a sign in their pediatric ER that reads "ONLY STABILIZING PROCEDURES ARE PERFORMED."

They prefer to blame stuff on inanimate objects, frequently. For example, if a teenager has an automobile accident, immediately they state "drugs must have been involved."

If their daughter has Grave's Disease related to extreme undue stress brought on by a faulty government and plain out harassment as well as neglect on their own parts, they become medical professionals. That does not surprise me in this town because I cannot believe that some of the unethical, immoral, and untrained nurses and doctors still are allowed to practice despite their clear and convincing negligence in my eyes. Instantaneously, I am accused of doing drugs for bulging or sunken eyes and I am also indicted and convicted of "screaming too much" for the loss of my voice. Despite the fact, some people have no idea what I ingest for food, they blame poor nutrition on other symptoms. This group appears to be real intelligent.

I found it necessary to utter these undeniably true facts not only because the rest of us are fully aware of them and they appear not to be in strict denial of such, but also it proves my point. Even though everyone knows someone like this, the remarks and labels (no matter how true) are hurtful and unnecessary. The remarks are akin to the labels that are inflicted and imposed on my child, Charlie Hart.

***The "Politicians"**—They are just like diapers; they are all dirty and change out frequently to other groups. These individuals are awesome double-talkers. They say one thing and do another and can frequently be caught talking out of both sides of their mouth at the same time.

***The "Credit Advisors"**—In this group, you will find those folks who like to advise everyone they can that they are the "deserving creditors". The persons in this group often take credit away from others who are more creditworthy. Sometimes they put themselves into a position of receiving overdraft protection because they freely use that credit every chance they get. They are quite pleased in their endeavors as evidenced by that affirmation they search out from others.

***The "Guards" (aka Wardens)**—The people in this group do a lot of supervising and control. Their primary purpose in life is "abuse of power." Their job is to lock you up and throw away the key. The twisted beliefs that they embrace are that "you have demons in you" when you attempt to tell them what abuse you are receiving from others (including them). I refer to them as habitual violators as well because they sit in their office jingling those lock-up keys all the while looking the other way. Seldom do these people in this group ever learn what it is really like to be a functioning family member.

*The "Out-of-Towner's"—These members find it convenient to escape out of town whenever a family event arises. Frequently, they avoid embarrassing situations or family gatherings due to the fact that their actions have validated that they do so. They avoid confrontation for months to save face. Rarely are they seen at family functions, and they frequently blame their spouse for their absence. Despite their actions, they do emerge once or twice a year to make an appearance, all the while thinking that everyone else has a poor memory. Telephones are of little use to them because they never answer them and frequently take the receiver off the hook. Members of this group frequently can be seen smiling, arriving late, and leaving early. They do not like to be involved.

*The "Vegas Dealers"—This group holds all the cards or at least they assume they do simply because they strive to do so in every waking moment. They have straightforward rules: they deal all the cards and you shut-up. When walking on their turf, you never win. There is no talking except from the dealer; you express anything verbally and you are through, you lose, as far as they are concerned. The rules are pretty plain; they win or they don't play.

*The "Umbrellas"—This group holds everything over your head. Even those that are dead and gone are still blamed for their misfortunes. The people in this category have very good memories; they never forget a thing and they sometimes remember things that never existed. They are very creative.

Then there are the **"medical professional wannabes"**. These individuals in my family have taken a "hypocritical oath". You would think they would be more ethical and careful how they portray themselves. Other categories include:

***The "Tulip Walkers"**—They tiptoe around the truth and pretend they haven't a clue what you are talking about; they are synonymous with "innocent bystanders" and will vehemently deny their involvement in anything later discovered to have been caused by them or something they did behind your back.

***The "Brown Nosers"**—They are fake in that they will ultimately say one thing to your face all the while saying the opposite to your back; they are similar to the "professional mourners" in that they are indeed waiting for that funeral but they target only a select few whereas the "professional mourners" target anyone and everyone. This category prefers to let the auditors believe that they are in control, even though they really believe that they themselves are in control.

***The "Hush Hushers"**—This group is also known as the "saints" of the family. They are superhuman in that they do not sin and if they do, they make sure everyone else keeps it under wraps. They prefer to smell like roses all the time. Their houses are immaculate and they never have dirty laundry. Their laundry is spic and span.

As far as the Bible, they do not want to be confused with the facts. I suppose my parents stopped "preaching the familiar verses" to me so much when I started studying the Bible and realizing that they only wanted to say & hear verses that made them feel more righteous and superior.

Dad actually got to the point that he began to hang up the phone on me when I quoted the "rest of the verses". Not only that, he would refuse to answer the phone when I called him right back.

No one likes to be wrong, but in my family you cannot be right. (Unless of course you happen to fall in that category of "veteran management". I think all of those positions have been filled for a very long time. I never liked working in family management unless it was my own personal management or that of my children.) I really should rephrase "management" to "audits and control". That term seems more appropriate because usually when that audit & control department steps in to matters at hand, you have not asked for their help. (That would be "Guest Services" that provide help to others.) When the "audit department" steps in they are scrutinizing everything you do, trying to find fault in anything and everything, and they are offering their services when you didn't ask for their assistance. I have found that this department does not work well in the classified department because they do not like dealing with the help wanted. They simply do not believe in it. Their own strict policies forbid it; their sole purposes is audit, control, and impose sanctions.

There are innumerable times that I was mistreated emotionally, mentally, and physically. To me, my entire life has been a misfortune, despite my well-intentioned efforts, with the exception of my wonderful children; my children have given me a purpose in my life.

It is heart wrenching for me to continuously have others to come along and even suggest taking that precious God-given gift from me. It absolutely terrifies me. I am horrified to entertain the notion that my mother, my father, my husband, COBB COUNTY and my aunt dody, for that matter, have suggested ripping that very "JOY" from my soul when that has been my sole happiness in my life.

I have actually worked hard at being a fantastic mom only for some "control freaks" to want to tamper with my body. Offering someone all their options is one matter, but insisting someone be "sterilized" denotes that I am about as equal in their eyes as an animal getting spayed or neutered. Life should be a "celebration", not a "mourning". People mourn at funerals.

Speaking of funerals, I am surprised that the very ones who call others in the family "the professional mourners"(which I must humorously agree) don't see themselves as the "experienced managers". I am convinced that there are an elite few who have "managed" to do their best at controlling what everyone does in this family.

My brother Phil once told me, "He who dies with the most 'toys' wins". I only knew he felt that way because he expressed it in those terms. He, like a lot of people in my family, has what I term "selective memory and recollection". They tend to recall only events that are favorable to them at the moment.

And most importantly, our children are our future and how we mold them today will have an everlasting impact on our own lives soon after. *I am amazed to fathom incomprehensibly the "JOY" that a pregnant mother-to-be has no sooner to forget those days, as their child gets older. That one has always been hard to grasp for me. I hope that I constantly express that same adoration for my children that I expressed when they were being woven together in my womb. I never want them to be unsuccessful and I hope that when they get the "chance to sit it out or dance, they dance." Leanne Womack couldn't have made it clearer: I hope they still feel small when they stand beside the ocean and I desire for them to ride those waves in security knowing I will always be there for them every chance I get. Meatloaf couldn't have sung it more appropriately and they took the words right out of my mouth: for crying out loud, you know I love you.*

So as far as the word "STONEHURST" is concerned, I get two 2 for 1's and you are absolutely correct. "ST" "HER" "ONE" "HURT" "ST", "SHE" "SURE". As far back as I can remember, nothing has ever turned out right for me in the finale; not that I ever really counted on it in the first place.

Mistakenly, I have always assumed that as long as I work at existing and providing the best I could bestow to my family and my friends, that everything would be okay; I strive to create a healthy, loving environment for my family realizing that life is not a bed of roses. At 40, I see myself as a failure. As an adult, I used to believe that I was invincible, and I had mentally convinced myself that no one would ever "run over me" and "control my fate" as had occurred previously in my life.

I see that it is all about that American dollar sometimes despite the fact that the money ain't worth two cents.

Everyone is hoarding money whereas they should be noticing that love is like that toothpaste ad, "put your money where your mouth is!" They say money does not grow on trees; ah, but love should. There should be no "GAP," it should be just like JCPenney's proclaims, "IT'S ALL INSIDE."

Maybe that's what's wrong; love should radiate from the inside to the outside. Saying "I Love You" is not the same as showing "I Love You." Similarly, love & sex do not necessarily have to be related. You can't be devoted to someone without being committed, and you can be devoted and committed without sex in a relationship; by the same token, sex may occur in a relationship where one or both people are neither devoted nor committed. I think that would be difficult for me. Although, understand that "the sex ain't worth two cents either" unless genuine expression by gestures and language at ALL other moments in a relationship constantly say, "I Love You".

That principle applies to all relationships of every kind: spousal, parental, and friend. People convey love for others by means of several different ways. A few of my favorites are the following: actions that match words on a virtually consistent basis; taking the time to listen to what others have to say and being truly interested; helping others by first finding out what their needs are and second helping them to achieve their goals in any way you are able; giving to others in need when you see a need, not expecting a gain; being congenial equally remembering that the family is the foundation that sets precedence for your behavior.

Moreover, I am troubled by the way the economy "works" in our society today; the media can make a common item either valuable & scarce or plentiful & worthless. When it snows a few flurries, people empty grocery store shelves of milk and bread; two items that have allergic tendencies in my family. When a terrorist "attacks", there is a run on duct tape and plastic. When hurricane Katrina floods some of Louisiana, everyone appears at the gas stations and price gouging ensues. In my honest and maybe outspoken opinion, the economy is surviving at the control and command of whatever someone says is scarce whether it be fact or not. First we get oil from "Iraq," (what a long way to send fuel) then we obliterate their country. Then someone says we get fuel from "Louisiana" (of all places) and all of the sudden people panic.

I panic but for a "logical reason." How many years have bad weather and floods been ailing our country? Next thing you know there will be a run on cars with better gas mileage; then what, "bicycles"? I got gas because my children needed to get to school everyday. I must hand it to the President of this country; he is very clever in "boosting the economy." I have never seen anything like this before in my life. I stand to wager that if he said computers were going to be obsolete tomorrow, then all of them would be on back order and sold out at stores nationwide. I bet if the President of the U.S. exclaimed, "There is a shortage of marrying women & good mothers and there is an over abundance of women", then the divorce rate would decline & marriage would be on the rise. Marriage license costs would no doubt soar to record prices.

Yes, I agree. I am hurt that my husband does not care for us, and I am upset that my family has no time for me. I am saddened it does not concern my husband whether or not we have shelter. Bothered by his failure to support our children and I, as evidenced by his abandonment, hurts due to the fact he is aware we are homeless, penniless, and destitute. He has not attempted to do anything about anyone's living situation but his own. I am hurt because I feel used by "Chuck" and some members of my own "family." I am hurt that my children are losing their home. I am hurt that I have always been a "giver" and it seems, by actions, that a lot of people in my life are "takers." I am hurt that it is necessary to write this book in order to get my point across and it pangs me that in all probability, a majority of those "phonies" still won't care about "the blue one's." It troubles me that when I ask for a hug from my mother, she simply and quickly replies, "I can't." It devastates me that in order to get "fake affection" in my family, one has to be "receiving material things" from a family member. I cry when I see repetitive control patterns that are evident to all except the one actually doing the "controlling."

Despite how some have treated me, I still care deeply for them and would probably still lend a HAND if they were in dire need. It bothers me that I care more than most about more than I probably should according to some. I am disturbed by the fact that **I forgive**; yet, **they never forget**. It particularly distresses me in that the self-proclaimed "black sheep" in my family gene lines are the very ones who I see more eye-to-eye with on subject matters such as these.

Speaking of lovely places, I drove by a new subdivision in my neighborhood. The houses are currently priced at $700K upwards. They are BEA-U-tiful. The houses are made of brick, stone, wood, and copper. Each house has a double front door and some have a pool. I noticed the lots numbered 1 & 5 are still vacant. I do not see a community playground for children and I think they should have one at those inflated prices. Perhaps a play area could be built on Lot 1. I fancied owning a house on lot 5. "5" **is** my favorite number because it is the number of grace and it happens to look like an "S." What's more is Lot # 5 seems like it is on a hill, and I do feel like I am on top of the world, sometimes. My desire was to build a similar house here at 3624 Trickum Rd. I hopelessly acknowledge that we won't live on Lot #5 either. The subdivision name flooded my eyes with tears. The subdivision's name is "STONEHURST." As I do read into things a lot, I saw "UR" "ST", "THERES ONE U ST." Aimee pointed out a decryption I elected to omit from **what** I deciphered in that word: "ST" "UR" "HURT ONE" or "UR ONE HURT ST."

A crossing sign the D.O.T. erected in our yard aligns with my car door when I park in the drive-way. Odd, however, an imaginary triangle forms once you mark the site of the lightening ball my daughter and I saw in front of our fireplace in our living room. One line is missing, but that is where the 2/1 = 3/1. At the cross, at the cross, where I first saw the light, I pray the burdens of my heart will roll away. By **faith**, there, I received **my sight**, literally, because I now read in far-fetched manners. Proclamation of my son's life delights me even though I still have remarkable memories of the event and a sum total lot of unanswered grief.

I wondered all the while if she knew that you should not have X-Rays if you may be pregnant, while I informed her that menstruation does not prevent pregnancy. Judging from the dumbfounded look, she may not have done the pregnancy test if I had not made that remark and requested one for my daughter.

Although nothing was done about it, I commented about the dirty floor. I reported the impersonal "bitch" at the check-in counter behind the waiting room door who "yanked" our papers from my hand and subsequently talked nasty to me right before she "barked" for security. How dare her "snatch" papers from me while I was writing on them. As a rule, I never sign blanket consent forms, because many doctors and nurses, particularly at that hospital, do not employ the practice of informed consent. Someone did FINALLY return my call. Yet, I never received a return call from Linda Clark, the hospital's administrator regarding my dissatisfaction with my children's' previous two visits. I told Mr. Westgate, "I would rather DIE than go to that hospital ever again and I contracted an eye infection from the unclean room. A week later, all my children became sick." I guess he had hoped to placate me by conducting an "environmental services walk through" as he termed it. In the mail, I received a BS letter that thanked me for visiting and it stated they had done the "walk through inspection". The findings were omitted. My strong recommendation is this: "STEER CLEAR OF WELLSTAR UNLESS I OWN IT," Evidently, I support patient rights and a definite name change of that hospital to "CHOICE HEALTH SYSTEMS." Go figure. Thank God there are more lovely places to visit in my town.

That is genuine true love and it is an example of how the "money ain't worth two cents." Somehow, God must have known that I needed that "kiss", and He sent it by way of Scott Rickles. I guess like the Ally McBeal's soundtrack song lyrics read, which originated from the TV series "Ally McBeal", "It's in his kiss". I loved the "dancing baby" and I never really contemplated whether or not Ally was nuts. I understood her perfectly; okay, I thought she was a little screwy but it is what engrossed me in the show. I was fond of the "Barry White" songs as well. Besides, I saw "decent attorneys" on the show; they were creative, ingenious, resourceful, and original. None of those are to be found from where I come; if there is one, I have not found him or her as of yet for my current quest. I have been seeking an attorney, for a year at least. The more days that pass, the more I paint a picture of purported negligence. I won't rebut such doctors, nurses, and lawyers were educated for many years. Yet, some are still deficient in intellectual acuity. It appears they became less educated and more injudicious.

After transporting my eldest girl to that same hospital that I detest (WellStar Kennestone Hospital), per her choice and selection due to proximity, I believe she will never select that hospital for a second time. What a nightmare! Besides the floor being soiled, black, & filthy in the pediatric ER, a health "professional" stated, "X-Rays aren't cumulative." Begging to differ, I educated her to the fact "X-Rays are identifiable potent mutagens." In asking her how the body purges X-Rays, she replied, "I don't know but they do." Reeducating her, I provided basis for the badges techs wear that keep track of exposure to radiation.

It was Christmastime one year and I was living at 2825 Okawana Drive in Marietta, Georgia, same county of Cobb. Sometimes they gave you 2 for 1 in that street name as it was commonly misspelled "Okawanna" and sometimes it was written Oakwanna"; the D.O.T. utilized all of those spellings for the signs on that street. Moving along with the memory, the doorbell rang and as I opened the door I saw Scott there as he stood with a giant Hershey's Kiss. I know my eyes bulged, as they were fixated on this larger-than-life size chocolate Hershey kiss in a box. For a child, it was colossal to say the least. All I can recall is my memory of asking whom it was for only to appreciate that he had gifted it to me. Although his actions were not prognosticated, I have not forgotten that act of benevolence. Even today, it remains a fond memory. Funny, the things we do remember and the impressions that remain in our minds.

I offered to give Scott a laptop that I own to use for his "baseball trips" to Cuba. Chosen for their beautiful churches, he has a mission in which he coaches baseball to underprivileged children in Cuba. He and his Mexican wife Rocio speak Spanish fluently which helps. He requested that I just hang on to it for now which so befuddled me.

We do need more computers in our home, but that one fits his needs and not ours. I hope he does eventually accept it because I truly want him to have it. I presumably hope he is cognizant of that. I en**JOY** doing for others e**SPECIAL**ly when I know they appreciate it. I will donate an entire day to those who value me as an individual, partly due to his one act of benevolence to me as a child in which he notably inked me with a demonstrable blueprint.

The lyrics to the song are printed below on this page. I did not want to omit a single stanza because I indubitably want to alert the world that **"this is my story, this is my song"** when they "follow the yellowbrick road" in this tome. For this book indeed will exist as a part of the final creation of my series of first books which will bear the title,

<u>The Chronicles Of Jess</u>.

Blessed Assurance

Blessed assurance, Jesus is mine!
O what a foretaste of glory divine!
Heir of salvation, purchase of God,
I'm born of His Spirit, washed in His blood.

Refrain:
This is my story, this is my song,
Praising my Savior all the day long;
This is my story, this is my song,
It's praising my Savior all the day long.
Perfect submission, perfect delight,
Visions of rapture now burst on my sight;
Angels descending bring from above
Echoes of mercy, whispers of love.

(Refrain)
Perfect submission, all is at rest;
I in my Savior am happy and blessed,
Watching and waiting, looking above,
I'm filled with God's goodness; I'm lost in His love.

(Refrain)

I do hope my book saves "a race, g." That is "grace" and you get a 2 for 1 on the "a".

The song playing on one of my favorite and most listened to radio stations, 104.7 The Fish began to play, *"It's All About Saving Grace."*

They ought to rewrite that song for my so-called family and my so-called friends; the new name for the song ought to be *"It's All About Saving Face."* You got me turning all around like the song lyrics read in "Turning Japanese." I have been listening to lyrics all day on one station or another. The station I have been listening to for the most part other than 104.7 The Fish, today, is Kicks 101.5. Sometimes, I like country music, and besides, they are giving away free gas credit cards. In itself, it is an incentive to alternate radio stations, given the fact that the price of gas has been grossly inflated recently.

I have for the most part been tuning in to 104.7 The Fish lately; more to the point, that radio station is a dearly loved and treasured favorite for my children and I. My son waves his hands towards heaven while enjoying the music.

One of our favorite songs is **Blessed Assurance**. I can just about recognize my cousin Scott Rickles voice singing that very song so plainly in my mind. He has a magnificent singing voice; I only wish I could sing as BEA-U-tiful like he does.

The *Next Day Savior CD* has the best version, other than my cousin Scott Rickles of course. I always did like Scott and will never forget the lasting impression he made on me as a child. I will never fail to remember it. I ponder if he recalls the incident, and I cogitate in my mind if he knows the selfless impression, kind sentiment, and enduring sensitivity while it has good-naturedly ordained me.

He said "Oh," and in retrospect I should have said, "I aM Oh, Oh God." I decided to choose my quips and not tackle that one. I noticed the phone company sign and read it also. It read, "Me come Por ST." "Por" means "for" in the Spanish language. There should be two o's in por because I am "poor." I also read "some more SDWT." You see I used the "m" 3x and once I reflected and flipped it. There is a 2 for 1 on the O's. "O O God, again, Mom". There is a lot of "geometric/algebraic reading" occurring in my brain. As I began to turn 40 years of age, my brain started scrambling the words that I read. My brain turned dyslexic all of the sudden, or at least my occipital lobe went into overdrive.

Math smarts do run in the family. I viewed a high action movie last night about space, astronauts, and James Bond. It was right up my alley. The movie was titled as such: ***"Moonraker" James Bond 007***. My husband likes "action", but he does not like me to say, "O O God." That's what I call myself for a variety of reasons. My girls look like clones, and my son looks like a fertilized clone. He arrived right on time for a fertilized clone, 230 days. Anyways, I read," **'OO' name 'OK'"** in that word when I employed the jingle: **"RR Crossing watch out 4 cars, CAN U SPELL without any R's?"** You get 2/1 and 3/1 in that word. My husband does not like the way I read and he gets irritated when I say, "O O God," unless I say it during a sexual encounter. Well, I guess he gave me a 2 for 1. Hmm, he has double standards also. U know Y, now, I use the term. **Natural cloning** and **decoding languages** are my specialty and miracle gifts. Hence, I say I am an **"O O God"** (for my eggs) and I am **"a girl named Yes."**

My parents as well as my siblings quoted such adages as "Life is unfair", "You reap what you sow", "If you lay down with a dog, you will get up with fleas", and so forth. I guess they should have realized that I was somewhat dyslexic and I read "dog" as "God."

I looked at my odometer; it read 101. If I chose to read between the lines, it could be a "zero" but there's no "zer," in that number. I know there can only be one "o" in "God." I like "O O God" but there is a 3 for1 (a gain) in that, and there is a 2 for 1 in "O God." God is good but there is **just one** "O" in God.

I stopped at the "Chevron" and saw that "CH" "UR" ONE." It looks like "U" to a lot of people if they broaden their point of view; for narrow-minded people, they see it as a "V." Either way, I see a lot of narrow-minded people around my town and in my environment. Just because people do not read like I do, they think I am crazy. No, I am not crazy, but my children are on top of the world in my opinion, and that opinion is the only one that counts. Besides "CH" is what we call my son "for short"; yes, pun is intended. And **Chevron is right** there is only **One Charlie Hart.** (See F.Y.I.)

I continued to drive my car to the phone company because I usually have to pay in person. I utilize metroPCS for phone service. They were closed and there were wires "hanging loose" at the door. I do not know why. But there did appear to be a slight problem with the door. Someone approached me as I opened the door and he said, "sorry Ma'am we are closed." I reached out my hand, passing the envelope with my payment as I said, "Just wanted to drop off a payment," as I granted him a smile.

That is what a family is supposed to do right? As I continued to drive, I noticed other 2 for 1's coming in as double standards.

Anyway, on Chastain Rd, a local street in this so-called town, I passed 2 speed limit signs that read, "35mph." Funny thing, I saw 1 on the other side of the road, same area. There, the speed limit sign read, "45mph." Anyways, I guess that is why people who "pay attention" to all the signs and to all that is going on around them while they are driving may be given a ticket for speeding. Because if they were looking "left" and saw the speed limit sign that read "45 mph," then the ones on the right side would not be seen. What if a far-sighted person was switching lanes from right to left and noticed the wrong sign? What an illegal thing to do by the county, in my opinion, since signs in the same area read "35 mph." Unfair I suppose, but someone will inevitably receive a speeding ticket for those contradictory signs.

The sign in the area read, "Construction zone" but it was 10:05 a.m. on a clear day and I saw no construction. As a matter of fact, I have been in that area at all times of the day and night, as well as early morning hours, and never ever have I seen anyone constructing anything. See what I mean? But like they say, "Life is unfair." I learned that concept at a very young age.

For one reason or another, no one had time and no one has agreed to take the case. One lawyer said, "Nothing's a slam dunk." I told him I talk to people in Cobb County daily and also I have lived here for forty years and I know that in a trial by jury we would win. I see a multi-billion dollar lawsuit with virtually every law having been violated and NO ONE HAS THE TIME! No one wants to prevent the judges, the attorneys, the department of family and children services, and the hospitals and doctors from **MISTREATING** a family like us ever again!

In my opinion, this goD-forsaken county and its "officials" as well as most of my family are "worthless, do-nothing networks." I am appalled and alarmed that networks such as these are allowed to exist in today's society; then again, nothing surprises me.

When I was a child, I felt lonely and abandoned by my family and other people as well. In my 40 years, I have discovered virtually no one cares at all. The few people who did care are still here. It seemed very "clear" to me.

Speaking of "clear," it was a clear day today and I saw a "no construction" sign as I was traveling down Chastain Rd., a local road in this so-called "county." I was reading the signs as usual and that is when I noticed, "sometimes signs are incorrect." See again, sometimes people are wrong, right? I know "opposites attract and still stand beside each other."

They drug tested my breast milk without my consent or knowledge according to my review of my son's medical records after they medicated my son with narcotics due to what appears to be an iatrogenically caused anaphylactic reaction to a drug called penicillin. I was not even a patient at their facility, but I had to leave my milk for my son while I fought their unethical and immoral actions in juvenile court. Those negative drug test results on my breast milk were then given out to several agencies in my county without my consent or knowledge.

I was totally unaware of these actions for at least 6 months as I only learned of them when I fought to get my son's medical records.

When I learned of these infractions, I also discovered that they had broken the O.C.G.A. law by extracting my son's DNA (again without our consent), a protected identity material under the Georgia law. (To my knowledge, four states including Alaska, Colorado, Florida, and Georgia currently have state statutes declaring genetic information to be personal property.) Subsequently, they dispersed these karyotype results to other agencies and government officials as well. As a result, my son was labeled "mentally retarded" and has suffered much damage; our family has suffered as well. I have had medical malpractice attorneys say, "there's not enough money in it." The medical mal attorneys also referred me to civil rights lawyers. I failed to locate a HIPAA attorney as well.

I heard my brother Tim say that to me, but he has "double standards" cause he "cain't" talk to me. I am AbeL why Cain't he be? I think he was right even though he was wrong; **it is in the writing.** It's actually in the signs, the writing, and the math: the 3 R's: reading, riting, and rithmetic. The A & W is missing, I know, I never did like root beer. YOOHOO is my favorite. You get a clone in that word. Two "OO"'s, but still one God, though. Same God, just 2 "O O's". O O God

That is when it finally occurred to me that the money was not worth two cents. I know my children are worth more to me than ALL the money in the world. I tried to find an attorney in my town for my son and my family, and I even looked to the outskirts of my town in other parts of the state; not one attorney was willing to take my case! I know a lot about the law, left and right, up and down; I read it all ways always. I think that I have a potential lawsuit involving claims of medical malpractice, assault & battery, false imprisonment, civil liberties violations (especially the 14th amendment to the pursuit of happiness for more than one occurrence), false swearing, kidnapping, violations of court orders, violations of due process, violations of freedom of religion, violations of search & seizure, violations of protected private property, (under Article V), violation of Article VI and the right to a speedy trial (with it being within ten days for an infant), violation of Article VII (right to a trial by jury), Violation of Article VIII (cruel and unusual punishment, with more than one count), and false swearing among other violations. WellStar Kennestone Hospital in Marietta, Georgia could potentially be liable for at least 3 HIPAA violations that are valued at $250K a piece.

I am also concerned that my grandmother is in utter fear that if she does not fall under their control, then she will be at the mercy of a dreaded nursing home. That saddens me. I returned her call and I asked her to please look in the local phone book and find an attorney for me while she was in Toccoa, Georgia, where her other house is located. Her response was…"I do not have time." The only words that I heard ringing over and over in my head were, "**I don't have time.**" I never understood why she never had time for me when I really needed her. It always appeared to me that **"money"** (earning it, spending it, and making the most of it) was always more important than **ME**!

Speaking of money, has anyone noticed, "The money ain't worth two cents"? I was noticing my money one day and all the differences between "the change" and "the bills." I looked at the half dollar, the quarter, the nickel, the dime, and the penny; it all made "no cents" to me and seemed "senseless." I then looked at the bills: the one, five, ten, and twenty; that is all I needed to see. How come the serial numbers were arranged differently and the green seal was a different color ink and in a different spot on the bills, especially the twenties which had the same year and the same Federal Reserve location? I decided to rub the bills on a piece of white notebook paper. The ink came off! I thought, "What the hell is going on around here?" The ink is not supposed to rub off of the bills. Besides the fact that it added up, everyone looked relatively different directions; yet, they all look related. Abe faces one way on the penny, but then he looks the other way on the 5. Sounds like my mother, but looks like my father. Abe L. looks like my dad; there are no CAINT'S around my house.

Chapter 3: "Y" Is For YELLOW

"Y" Everyone Should Be "Seen & Heard"; Everyone Has A Choice: Now U C "Y"

My mother is such a bitch. I would not be surprised if she does not talk to me at all (again) because I wrote that in a book; go figure. I really would not be any worse off than I am right now. That is so old hat that I could write a popular song about it. Sometimes it does take a doG to run a kingdom, but sometimes that same doG can ruin a kingdom.

My mother rarely calls me and when she does, she either wants me to look up names, addresses, and telephone numbers for her, or she is so busy talking about herself that I would be surprised if she even knew I was still on the other end of Ma Bell. Sometimes calling people with exciting news about ourselves is normal, but it disturbs me that my mother gets more excitement out of her "issues" and her "cows" as opposed to her family. That really bothers me.

My mother called me twice last week. She wanted to know how to perform an Internet search and she also wanted me to check up on my grandmother, Mama Teen for her because she was out of town in Toccoa and "could not check on her"; I guess she was too busy with her "bull", or maybe she had already used her precious minutes; God only knows.

I am doing a genetic family tree to inform others what wonderful gift genes there are in my family and what miraculous things happen despite all the disease we also have. Strange, but all the ones who carry those diseases, with which they will die without the help of my doctor, are not interested in helping me with my genetic family tree. I think I know why.

I was really confused by that one because he says, "No one ever comes to see (him)."

Mostly, my parents just hang up when they are done talking, as does my sister. She has limited talk time on her phone also. I always wonder how they know I am still on the other end of the phone because I never get a chance to say much. I also wonder how they know so much about my condition and my son's intelligence when they neither ask nor visit. Maybe they go to the same doctors that cared for my son in the hospital. Those doctors took one look at my son's genes and they swore he would be mentally retarded. Those doctors seemed to also be suffering from the same diseases that some of my "family" and "friends" are being debilitated by daily.

The only time I see my family is when I go to their house. The only time they call is when they want to tell me how cute their cow is and how they cannot wait to have another. My parents call when they need their car fixed or when they just want to meddle and control someone. As a matter of fact, my mom needs her bumper fixed with touch up paint, and she wondered if Chuck could get her some. I was slightly confused on that, also, because she wanted to force Chuck to leave and get the house quit claimed to me. In addition, she wanted to "sterilize" me in order for her to help me save my home.

I know a lot about my family and friends and I tried to tell them all about what I enjoy doing and the research in genetics that I am doing now.

My children probably will not be in the same great district that we are in right now because we will be living in a shelter somewhere or a week-to-week motel room; so, I will probably continue to deteriorate health wise with Grave's Disease. But that does not bother me. It only bothers me that I gave up some of my great gene gifts to a public school system in which I do not like only to give my children a roof over their head, in hopes of searching for a job because my husband is not providing like he used to.

I am also bothered that I was going to share my great gene gifts with my so-called family and friends, and then, I got tearful when I found out what they really thought about my children. What a shame, they will die with stupidity, hate, and a high self-worth. At least, I know when they die, they will die being a supreme being. I am happy for them that they think so highly of themselves; who am I to judge. I know my doctor will see their worth one day. I guess I should have told them this too, but they always cut me off when they are finished talking because of one reason or another. Usually, it is because they cannot afford to talk to me because they have limited minutes on their phone (and they used them all up when they were talking).

Sometimes, my dad says he has to go see his wife's family or go to a funeral or something. That is what he said when he rushed me out of his home last time he invited me to visit.

I have a lot of faith in my doctor and wondered if he could cure the disease that all of the people I spoke with that same day shared.

It seemed to me that they all had the same debilitating disease with a variance here and there. He again assured me that my "special gene gift" could cure their disease. I told my doctor that I could not get a commitment from any of them to accept my gift. My doctor offered to speak with my family and friends, but I said you would hear the same thing when you speak to them. One minute they will tell yes they want the gene, and then in the same breath they will say they do not accept it. My doctor told me he will speak to them personally, but he cannot make them listen or accept my gifts or me.

I was so saddened because I knew these very people were going to die with this disease that seems to take many forms. I could almost hear some disappointment in his voice, but I prayed and begged my doctor to please make them accept. I know my prayer this time will go through; my doctor said it would. I know it will go through because my doctor is God. The diseases that he can cure are superiority complex, stupidity, supremacy, ascendancy, control, and prejudice. I am so glad that I learned these things about some of the people in my life. I now know that I will lose my home and I will probably not get a job until my son Charlie Hart turns three when he can get enrolled in the public school system.

His added comment, as I told him I was losing my house and I did not know what to do, was that I should go live in a shelter. In his same breath, he told me that he would be go camping with the Sam's Club in his motor home. I was so happy for him and wanted to hear all about it when he returned. Naturally, I asked (as I do every time) how his trip was and also how he was doing with all the debilitating disease he had. He was happy to tell me all about all his problems and his vacations. I asked if I could do anything to help him and of course again I told him as well that I wanted to share my "special gene gift" with him. He seemed contradictory, as did my mother and a lot of my "friends." I was getting quite confused and was trying to figure out if they wanted my "God given gene gift" or not. After all, my doctor is the greatest well-known doctor of all time.I told my family and friends that he had been healing people for a long, long time, so long that the people of this age and time referred to him as "Healer." My mom was concerned about all the "New Age" beliefs as she termed it that she said she did not want to discuss it. Besides, she was so excited about her new baby calf that she had to go and hung up on me while I was still talking.

Much to my surprise, my dad should have been a doctor; too, because he says he knows that an extreme level of undue stress does not bring about Grave's Disease. I wondered why he was not my doctor. When I asked my doctor, he again assured me there was only one in the world like him.

My parents and my friends know that I am a giving person, and above all, I love and give to my own children all my love. I told my friends and parents in this same conversation that I would love to have 10 more just like them, especially like Karla Michelle, Mazur Gemini, Charlese Star, and Charlie Hart. Charlie Hart was my only child "labeled" Down Syndrome, a genetic condition resulting in extra genes. Knowing my age and Charlie's diagnosis, I was very surprised that "my parents" and "friends" told me that I probably should not have any more children. My mother offered to "pay off my house if I got 'sterilized'", and stated, "(she) would also pay for the surgery." One of my sister-in-laws remarked, *"YOU ARE KIDDING!"* when I told her, "If I could have 10 more like Charlie, then I would sign up now." A friend of my husband's (who allows my husband to fix his car for free or near free, and then he borrows his car to boot so he will have a car to drive) just had a baby and wants more because his son is so cute. I asked him if I told him I was pregnant with a boy exactly like Charlie, what would his recommendation be. He replied, "That is so stupid that you ask a question like that. Of course, you would have an abortion." My mom states that she can assist in babysitting my children while I search for work, but she does not have time for me. My father is remarried to a woman who has a Down Syndrome grandchild. He says he will take the girls and watch them a few days but he cannot watch Charlie.

My doctor, being Christ like himself, then continued to quote scripture to me.

"God can still provide a child even in our old age."
Genesis 17 and 18 "...Abraham and Sarah were old and well stricken in age; and it ceased to be with Sarah after the manner of women...."
Genesis 37:3 "Now Israel loved Joseph more than all his children, because he was the son of his old age..."
Luke 1:5-20, 36 "...Zacharias...[and] Elisabeth...had no child, because that Elisabeth was barren, and they both were now well stricken in years.... she hath also conceived a son in her old age..."

I started to sigh as I had been quoted bible scripture my whole life from my parents; they still quote it today. I had been doing my research in the Bible and I knew my doctor was absolutely right. After all, I also knew that in Genesis, God said, "...be fruitful and multiply." I had told my parents and a few of my "friends" that I was so excited that my doctor told me that I had the cure for a disease that a lot of people had. Most seemed curious, some unbelieving, and a few were excited (probably because they had this very disease).

When I told my friends and parents that I would be glad to share my genes with them to help cure their disease at no cost to them because I love and care for them so much, they did not know what to say but graciously accepted right away.

Chapter 2: "O" Is For ORANGE

My visit to the doctor

Wonderful news, my doctor has just informed me that my genes carry a cure for one of the fastest growing cancers in our society. When my doctor told me this, I was so elated, that tears came to my eyes. There was one catch, however; he told me that the cure could only come from a newborn baby. He had a long explanation for it that I could not even begin to repeat. He was well aware that I am 39 years old and suffering Grave's Disease. He assured me that even though pregnancy stresses the body that people as old as Methuselah, at 187 years, have had children. I told my doctor that some people fear that my husband and I (at our age 45 and 39) think that we should not have any more children. I asked, "What if I cannot have any more children and I am barren?" Again he assured me and referred to biblical reference quoting the following scriptures, since he indeed knew I am Christian:

He said: "They also bore children in old age." *Genesis 5:3 Adam, at 130 years; Genesis 5:6 Seth, at 105 years; Genesis 5:9 Enos, at 90 years; Genesis 5:12 Cainan, at 70 years; Genesis 5:15 Mahalaleel, at 65 years; Genesis 5:18 Jared, at 162 years; Genesis 5:21 Enoch, at 65 years. Genesis 5:25 Methuselah, at 187 years; Genesis 5:28, 29 Lamech, at 182 years; Genesis 5:32 Noah, at 500*

I know when I read the Bible, Jesus was in the middle of two criminals (hate on both sides with love in the middle). They were all hanging on reflectively, crosses. +.

As Jesus is love, he looked to either side and saw hate, but he stood up for what was right, right in the middle: One man, One cross, one right.

I always heard that two wrongs don't make a right, but maybe 2 wrongs do make 1 right; it did in my case. 2 for 1, right.

A lot of people think I am nuts, but I see a "su" "n" a "cross" in that. My husband says that I am "psycho." I told him, "cy" "SD's" "*40*"? Yes, I must be psycho, but most people interpret that word as "mentally disrupt." How could I be mentally bad? I am not bad, but g**oo**d. That is 2 o's in **god. I am** *Yes,* that's 2 S's. Kinda looks like *Zues,* but a different god. **God = good, right?**

I notice that the "sun" shines on me everywhere I go. Sometimes it rains, and sometimes I cry. I think if you read right, you now see all the Y's: **Big ones**, little ones, TALL ONES, & *short ones*, justice for ONE, justice for ALL, ALL for ONE and ONE for ALL. That means there are 3 = 1, and 1 = infinity. I hope you are one of the chosen ones; I hope you are in that number. If you can read everything I have written in all ways, then you are in that infinite number: that number **1, you are it.** I hope you see it, I hope you do, *cous*, there ain't no one quite like YOU.

I have to call after 7 pm because the minutes are free then. But if she does not like what I am saying, then she tells me she does not want to hear it and hangs up the phone. Face to face she puts her hand up to my face. In sign language that means "you-r" but in her language it means, "I am cutting you off, SHUT-UP." I cry when I see her treat me badly and I cry when I mirror it to my children. So when I see what I have reflected, I change it and make a difference. My children are the most valuable possession I have.

My mother has rewritten her will and left copies laying everywhere so many times that I feel nauseous. She eliminates someone different each time. Money is not where the love is. "The love of money is the root of all evil", my Bible says. Reflexively, it's the same. Money can't buy you love. That's Y-OU. She never learned that "the love in your heart wasn't put there to stay, Love isn't Love until you give it away." She never really helped me either way. Dad neither. I thought it took 2 to make 1 thing right? 4 1's in math are 1. She had 4 children and 1 turned out right. Maybe she did get 2 for 1 that time. She is a mathematician and she kept telling me, "It's in the NUMBERS." Did she mean the Bible Book NUMBERS, or did she mean the Math Book NUMBERS? Either way, it all adds up. Read them both, always; you will see it all ways. I know, there you got 2 for 1. Allways = Always. She was right on that too. She has a lot of right. That meant that 1 White was right, but how come I saw her wrong. Could right = wrong?

Could hate = love? Could me = you? Could 1 = 1?

I decoded the bible, because I am Zues, Yess I am; I know, there's an extra one. Sometimes I like blue eggs and ham.

My family never has time for me. I called my brother Tim and he said he had time for me, but as I got halfway thru the alphabet, he said, "Make it quick, I have to go." Then he added, "Some of us have to work for a living," and the phone went dead. The other day he told me, "It is all in the writing. That's where the money is at." Yet he had **no** time for me. That's **ono.** I do not understand. I keep putting all my time and effort into having a relationship with my family and it keeps failing me. I am not getting the love, care, and concern back, why? He says his blood type is +, but I say he's wrong, because he acts so negative…to me anyways, and I am O-. My other brother is O-like me but with an IQ of 144 (he says). If he's so smart, then why didn't **he** have time to listen to my short story? Why didn't he have time for me? He said he really didn't have time, but he spent as much time-if not more-arguing about how "it didn't matter" and "it doesn't make a difference" that he could have listened to my story probably twice; then he would have gotten 2 for 1. I don't see why I don't matter to him; everyone matters to me.

My mom cannot talk on the phone to me because she saves her minutes for more important things. What is more important than **ME**? I know I am less important to her than the rest of the kids. She even bought a house near Tim and they raise cows together. Those cows are more important than me. She spends a lot of time on her phone talking about cows, calves, and bulls.

DNA works the same way in that sometimes it flips and mirrors the other. Sometimes the mirror flips the reflection and it comes back to you. You read it all ways, up & down, left 2 right, and right 2 left. The code is individual, yet we were all created in His image. We were all created like **1**, One God! We are all **one**, just like the **3** in 1.

They say identical triplets are impossible, but they are not. It's just like the 3 in 1. Reflect what you see, flip it, reflect it again and come back to you. There's the 3rd one. It's all the same code, but all a different code, just like the trinity.

They say that multiples have the same DNA. Yes and No. There's always a difference, always **one** difference. It's there in the DNA code. The code is just slightly different. That's what makes us all different, yet all the same, all the shades of gray in between.

I looked at my Chex mix. There were breadsticks, corn & wheat squares, pretzels, clusters, etc…I always add M&M's because I like variety and I want all the colors. I use all the color M&M's…blacks, whites, purples, pinks, greens, yellows, oranges, reds, and even the blue ones. I would like to see chartreuse, periwinkle, and all the other colors, but if you add blue M&M's you can see all those other colors. Just like JeSus loved all the little children of the world: Red & Yellow, Black & White. What's missing? The **blue** ones. Someone said there were no blue babies, but yes there are, and without blue all the colors of the rainbow are not there. There are no purple or green. We must have **all** the colors in order to exist: all the colors, all the DNA, all the disabilities, all the differences, or we cannot exist together as one, just as our God intended.

K for Karla Michelle
J for Just ME
I for individualism
H for Here WE are
G for GOD go get 'em and Gemini
F for First Place
E for Excellent
D for Diversity
C for Caring and Charlie Hart and Charlese Star
B for Beautiful and Being who they are
A for Awesome and A<u>mazing</u> Grace

I taught my children some of all languages: sign language, because signs are everywhere just like labels; body language, because we all put off signs and we all have one; and many foreign languages because we all are foreign and that means we all Reign foR. I know 2 R's, but you get 2 for 1 in that word. Sometimes you get two for 1. Sometimes you get the same thing every time; they call that a **clone**, but c you're still <u>**A**</u> lone. That's an **A** in my book.

They labeled my son "Down Syndrome" and said "I'm sorry, he has extra 2 1." Why were they sorry? I read it differently. He has extra <u>**us**</u>, extra <u>**2 for 1**</u>, **extra Oh O*H* God.** God, that reminds me, I am 4O. O*H*. Well, the DNA works the same way. When my brother had triplets, one was reflective of the other, and then the third was reflexive coming back to you just like mirrors. Take a mirror and sit in your car, either side will do ya. Then, see the side view mirror reflect into the window? Hold another mirror up and face the mirror. Do you see all the different people? They are all you, every one of them! They are all related, and they all come back to one, just one, je su<u>i</u>s, I am. I am ma.

We grade people and send a grade home that denotes who they are. The child with the label of "**S**" will think they are just "satisfactory" and not "SUPER." If they receive an "F" they are "failed" and not "forgiven" or maybe it means they didn't learn what they should have in the **f**irst place, with "**F**" being in the **f**irst grade. Actually, when you look at it they are in LAST place when "**F**" stands for first.

I looked around and saw all these **Y**'s and wondered y? **Y**-ou? Why do people label others and why do I have to explain? What difference does it make what color you are, what sexual preference you have, how you style your hair, or how you keep your papers arranged in your house? As for me, my house is too small for my family. We learn a lot of stuff, so we have a lot of stuff. I give them a "z" for "zummi", an "F" for failing to pick up their stuff, and an "F" for "First Place."

I give them a:

Z for Zummi, I am Zeus
Y just because of **Y**ou
X means Mark the spot
W for we stand for Justice, that's two U's for Us
V for very well done
U for All of US
T for Thank You
S for **ME**/Star
R for Really, you need your rest now
Q for QT
P for Please
O for OO God
N for Naughty, but Nice
M for Mazur
L for Love

Chapter 1: "R" Is For RED

DECODING THE LANGUAGE

As I decoded the languages, I found different ways of looking at things. I wondered about labels and why they read the way they did. Why did we as humans label packages and people? Do we label so we know what we are getting? For instance, do we label someone "dyslexic" because they do not read like the rest of the population? Or do we label people dyslexic because they read better than the rest of us? When someone acts different than someone else, we put a label on that person, and then like mathematics teaches us we learn to group those people together. Isn't that what we learn to do in school? After all, don't we learn that "birds of a feather flock together?" Why can't we have an "invitation to come as you are?" Why in public schools are people labeled **A, B, C, D, E, F, S, US, and NS?** A= you score 100 according to someone's scale of zero to a hundred with 100 being the top score. Why can't **0** or **1** be the top score? Why not **5**? Why not **10**? Sometimes a **10** is perfect and an **11** is master. That all depends on how you read it. "**F**" means "failing," but in whose eyes? Maybe I have failed you, but not failed myself. How come in elementary school "**E**" = **Excellent** but it comes between a "**D**" and an "**F**"? How come "**US**" stands for justice for all, United States, and us together but in a child's life we teach them it stands for "unsatisfactory"? **S** stands for a lot of things like sun, *YES*, and Sue, but in a child's primary life we teach them it stands for just "satisfactory."

Shirley once told me, "Don't Thank ME, Thank God"; thus, I am thanking Her as well. Without God, the possible would have been impossible and I may never have seen the light at the end of that dark tunnel.

40 years have come and gone
and NOW I must STart on 40 1.
May God send YOU ALL the signs
U need 2 read,
Because I love YOU ALL, Y
-OU ALL InDeed.
Each & Every ONE thaTS come
ALL for 1, ONE 1 for ALL. I'm done.

compilations of stories as I wrote them; for they did not complain, and only did the care of a child come before my babbling.

Mark Jonathan Hand, Nancy Kracula Eggersman, Jeffrey Steven Heatwole, Ayoca Freeman, Shirley Cook, Michael Champion & his welcoming family (Colleen, Nathan, Chris, Michele, & Edith) including Bernie Cather, and Aimee LeBeuf CHIASSon: without Aimee I would not know the answer to the question "Where's The Beef?" Special Thanks for motherly advice goes to my dearest neighbor, Doris Rose McCurdy.

I find it necessary to send a BIG HUG & THANK YOU again to all of the Champion family for they embraced my children and I in when no one else would and gave us a loving home when we were homeless; they are indeed the "CHAMPIONS."

I do not want to leave out the less fortunate members of my "family" and my "friends" for all the times that "someone" or "something" was more important than ME: all the "saved minutes" and all the "Bull" has a lasting impression on me that I will never be able to forget.

FOREWORD

Sometimes it's backwards to be forward, and sometimes being bold, assertive, blunt, and outspoken is the way to speak UP and OUT to some people. Sometimes there is more than ONE WAY to go and sometimes that U turn is my turn to go 180 degrees and your turn-to-turn 180 degrees so that we may go full circle, 360 degrees. I end up 1st that way, usually. (There is an "I" in "1st".) So, even though my foreword is last, sometimes those in last place are placed first.

"All My Children" (eSPECIAlly Charlie Hart, Charlese Star, Mazur Gemini, and Karla Michelle-HAND it to them) always are first place in my book.

Without my "family" and my "friends" this book would not be possible; for without their somewhat insane behavior, I would not have been sane enough to write this book.

I want to say: "kam sa ham ni da," "Dhanyabad," "Shukriya," "Mahalo," "Toda," "Merci," "Grazie," "Danke," "Dank u," "Gracias," "Arigato": a big Thank Y-OU to all the true "amigos" who sat and listened to my endless chapters and short

These are my four children: Charlese Star, Karla Michelle with Charlie Hart, and Maze.

978-0-595-37775-6
0-595-37775-0

Printed in the United States
56958LVS00003B/99